The Tale of Halldor Snorrason II

Original Text, Translations, and Word Lists

Translated by Matthew Leigh Embleton

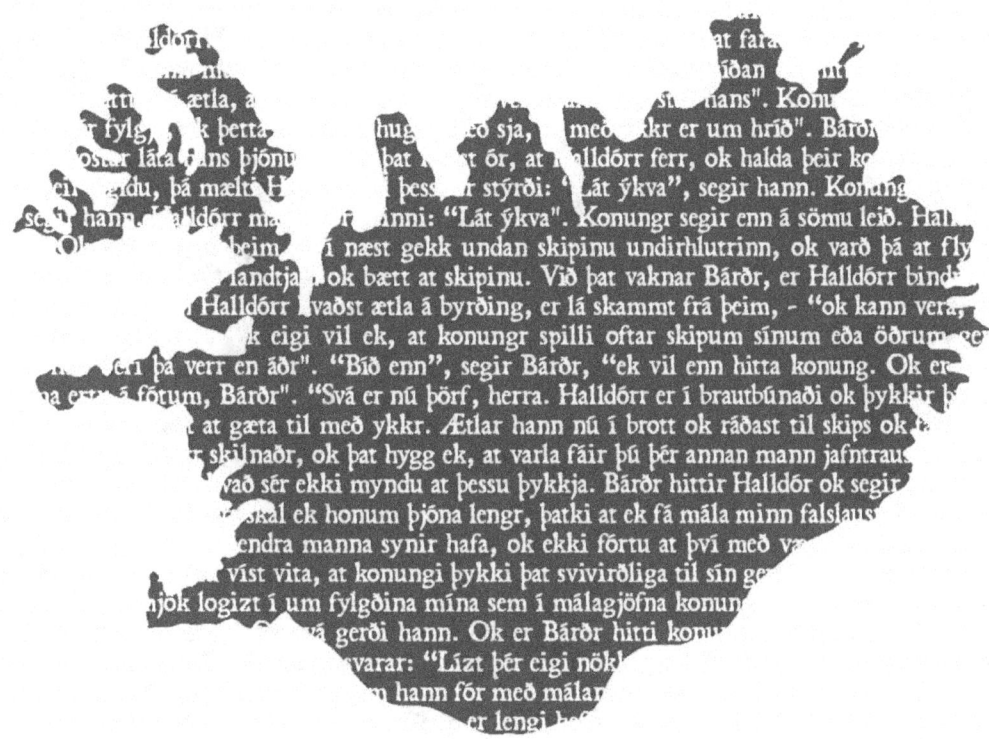

Copyright ©2025 Matthew Leigh Embleton. All rights reserved.

The Tale of Halldor Snorrason II

The Tale of Halldor Snorrason II (*Old Norse*)..4
Word List *(Old Norse to English)*..26
Word List *(English to Old Norse)* 39
The Tale of Halldor Snorrason II (*Old Icelandic*) 50
Word List *(Old Icelandic to English)* 72
Word List *(English to Old Icelandic)* 85
A Word Comparison of Old Norse and Old Icelandic Words 96

Cover: Old Norse text over an outline of Iceland. Author's design.

The original Old Norse and Old Icelandic texts are in the public domain.
These translations ©2022 Matthew Leigh Embleton
©2025 Matthew Leigh Embleton (This Edition)

Acknowledgments

I have long been fascinated by languages and history, and I am very grateful to the special people in my life who have supported and encouraged me in my work. Thank you for believing in me. You know who you are.

Introduction

Old Norse is a North Germanic language spoken by inhabitants of Scandinavia from about the 7th to the 15th centuries. Old Icelandic is a variety of Old West Norse that emerged during the Norse settlement of Iceland in the second half of the 9th century. The rich tradition of Icelandic literature survived by oral tradition over several centuries before being written down in the 13th Century. The Tale of Halldor Snorrason II (*Halldórs þáttr Snorrasonar inn síðari*) is one of the many Tales of Icelanders or *Íslendingaþættir*. The word '*þáttr*' (plural: '*þættir*') translates as a strand of rope or a yarn, comparable to the word 'yarn' in English sometimes used to refer to a story.

This book contains:
- The Tale of Halldor Snorrason II (*Halldórs þáttr Snorrasonar inn síðari*) (Old Norse Version)
- An Old Norse to English Word List
- An English to Old Norse Word List
- The Tale of Halldor Snorrason II (*Halldórs þáttr Snorrasonar inn síðari*) (Old Icelandic Version)
- An Old Icelandic to English Word List
- An English to Old Icelandic Word List
- A Word Comparison of Old Norse and Old Icelandic words

The texts are presented in their original form, with a literal word-for-word line-by-line translation, and a Modern English translation, all side-by-side. In this way, it is possible to see and feel how the worked and how it has evolved. This book is designed to be of use and interest to anyone with a passion for the Old Norse or Old Icelandic language, Norse history, or languages and history in general.

The Tale of Halldor Snorrason II (*Old Norse*)

Old Norse	Literal	English
1	**1**	**1**
HALLDÓRR Snorrason hafði verit út í Miklagarði með Haraldi, sem áðr er sagt, ok kom í Nóreg með honum austan ór Garðaríki.	Halldor Snorrason had been out in The-Great-City with Harald, as before was said, and came to Norway with him east from Gardariki.	Halldor Snorrason had been to Constantinople with Harald as has been said before, and went east to Norway with him from the Kievan Rus'.
Hafði hann þá mikla sæmð ok virðing af Haraldi konungi.	Had he then much honour and worthiness from Harald the-king.	Then he had much honour and worthiness from king Harald.
Var hann með konungi þenna vetr, er hann sat í Kaupangi.	Was he with the-king that winter, when he stayed at Kaupang.	He was with the king that winter when he stayed a Kaupang in Skiringssal.
En er á leið vetrinn ok vára tók, bjuggu menn kaupferðir sínar snemma, því at náliga hafði engi eða lítill verit skipagangr af Nóregi fyrir sakar ófriðar ok aga þess, sem verit hafði milli Nóregs ok Danmerkr.	And when had passed winter and spring took, preparations people trading-voyages theirs early, because of nearly had none or little been shipping from Norway for the-sake-of hostilities and turbulence those, as had-been had between Norway and Denmark.	And when winter had passed into spring, people began preparations for trading voyages early, because there had been little in the way of trade from Norway because of hostilities and turbulence between Norway and Denmark.
En er á leið várit, fann Haraldr konungr, at Halldórr Snorrason ógladdist mjök.	But when that passed spring, found Harald the-king, that Halldor Snorrason un-glad much.	But when spring had passed, king Harald found Halldor Snorrason very unhappy.
Konungr spurði einn dag, hvat honum bjó í skapi.	The-king asked one day, what he settled in mood.	One day the king asked what had settled in his mood.
Halldórr svarar:	Halldor answered:	Halldor answered:
"Út fýsir mik til Íslands, herra".	"Out desire me to Iceland, lord".	"I desire to travel out to Iceland, lord".
Konungr mælti:	The-king spoke:	The king said:
"Margr myndi þó heimfúsari verit hafa, eða hver eru fararefnin, eða hversu verst fénu?"	"Many would though home-longing being had, but where are travel-goods, or how-so becomes wealth?"	"Many would be longing for home, but where are your travel goods, and how will you spend your wealth?"

The Tale of Halldor Snorrason II (Old Norse)

Old Norse	Literal	English
Hann svarar:	He answered:	He answered:
"Skjótt ætla ek at verja, því at ekki er til nema ígangsklæði mín".	"Swift intend I to spend, because that not have to take travelling-clothes mine".	"Swiftly it seems spent to me, because I don't have any travelling clothes to take".
"Lítt er þá launuð löng þjónusta ok margr háski, ok skal ek fá þér skip ok áhöfnina.	"Little is then repaid long service and many dangers, and shall I pay you a-ship and crew.	"Your long service and all its dangers are little repaid, and I shall buy you a ship and a crew.
Skal faðir þinn sjá mega, at þú hefir mér eigi til engis þjónat".	Shall father yours see may, that you have me not to nothing served".	Your father shall see that you have not served me for nothing".
Halldórr þakkaði konungi gjöfina.	Halldor thanked the-king the-gift.	Halldor thank the king for his gift.
Fám dögum síðar fann Halldórr konung, ok spurði konungr, hversu mjök hann hefði ráðit sér skipverja.	A-few days later found Halldor the-king, and asked the-king, how-so much he had hired for the-crew.	A few days later Halldor found the king and asked him how much of the crew had he hired.
Hann svarar:	He answered:	He answered:
"Allir kaupsveinar hafa sér ráðit áðr skipan, en ek fæ enga menn, ok því ætla ek, at eftir mun verða at vera skip þat, er þér gáfuð mér".	"All trading-men have themselves hired other ships, but I give no men, and therefore suppose I, that remaining should be that becoming the-ship that, is you gave me".	"All the traders have been hired by other ships, but I have got no men, and therefore I suppose that the ship that you gave me should remain".
Konungr mælti:	The-king spoke:	The king spoke:
"Eigi er þá vinveitt gjöfin, ok skulum vit enn bíða, hvat ór ráðist um háseta".	"Not is then favourable gift, and shall with then wait, what from decide about sailors".	"Then it is not a favourable gift, and with that we shall wait to decide about the sailors".
Annan dag eftir var blásit til móts í bænum ok sagt, at konungr vill tala við bæjarmenn ok kaupmenn.	The-next day after was trumpet-blown to meet in the-town and said, that the-king wished-to speak with townspeople and merchants.	The next day the trumpet was blown to meet in the town, and the king said that he wished to speak with the townspeople and the merchants.
Konungr kom seint til mótsins ok sýndist með áhyggjusvip, þá er hann kom.	The-king came late to the-meeting and seemed with worried-face, then as he came.	The king came late to the meeting and seemed to have a worried face when he arrived.
Hann mælti:	He spoke:	He spoke:

The Tale of Halldor Snorrason II (Old Norse)

Old Norse	Literal	English
"Þat heyrum vér sagt, at ófriðr muni kominn í ríki várt austr í Vík.	"This hear we said, that un-peace shall come in kingdom ours east about Vik.	"We hear this, that war shall come to our kingdom east in Vik.
Ræðr Sveinn Danakonungr fyrir Danaher ok vill oss vinna skaða, en vér viljum með engu móti upp gefa vár lönd.	Leading Svein King-of-Denmark for Danish-forces and wishes us to-win-over damages, but we wish-to with none meet up give our land.	King Svein of Denmark is leading the Danish forces and means to win over and damage us, but none of us wish to give up our land.
Fyrir því leggjum vér bann fyrir hvert skip, at ór landi fari, fyrr en ek hefi slíkt sem ek vil af hverju skipi, bæði af liði ok vistum, nema einn knörr, eigi mikill, er á Halldórr Snorrason, skal ganga til Íslands.	For therefore lay we a-ban before each ship, to out-of the-land travel, before that I have such as I wish from each ship, both of men and provisions, except one ship, not great, that of Halldor Snorrason, shall go to Iceland.	Therefore we lay a ban on each ship from travelling out of these lands, until I have what I wish from each ship, men and provisions, except for one small ship of Halldor Snorrason which will go to Iceland.
En þótt yðr þykki þetta nökkut strangt, er áðr hafið búit ferðir yðrar, þá berr oss nauðsyn til slíkra álaga, en betra þætti oss, at um kyrrt væri at sitja ok færi hverr sem vildi".	But though you think this somewhat strange, is before have prepared travel yours, then bears us necessity to such stress, but better seems to-us, that about peace was that settle and travel each as wish".	You will think this somewhat strange, when you have prepared your travel, but it this stress is necessary, and it would be better for us if there was peace and each man could travel wherever he wished.
Eftir þat sleit mótinu.	After that broken-up the-meeting.	After that the meeting was broken up.
Litlu síðar kom Halldórr á konungs fund.	Little afterwards came Halldor to the-king find.	A little afterwards Halldor came to find the king.
Konungr spurði, hvat þá liði um búnaðinn, hvárt hann fengi nökkura háseta.	The-king asked, what then crew about preparations, each he found some crew.	The king asked about what preparations had been made for some crew.
Halldórr svarar:	Halldor answered:	Halldor answered:
"Helzti marga hefi ek nú ráðit, því at miklu fleiri koma nú til mín ok beiða fars en ek mega öllum veita, ok veita menn mér mikinn atgang, at drjúgum eru brotin hús til mín, svá at hvárki nótt né dag hefi ek ró fyrir ákalsi manna her um.	"Rather many have I now hired, because that a-great more came now to me and asked travel than I may all lead, and grant people me much access, that greatly they violated house to me, so that neither night nor day have I rest for calling people here about.	"I have hired rather a lot of men, because a great more came to me and asked to travel than I may lead, and granted much access that my house is violated, so that I have no rest, neither day nor night for these people calling here abouts".

The Tale of Halldor Snorrason II (Old Norse)

Old Norse	Literal	English
Konungr mælti:	The-king spoke:	The king spoke:
"Haltu nú þessum hásetum, sem þú hefir tekit, ok sjám enn, hvat í gerist".	"Hold-you now those sailors, that". you have taken, and we-see then, what will be".	"Now keep the sailors that you have hired, and we will see what will happen".
Næsta dag eftir var blásit ok sagt, at konungr vill enn tala við kaupmenn.	Next day after was trumpet-blown and said, the king wished then speak with the-merchants.	The next day, a trumpet was blown, and it was said that the king wished to speak with the merchants.
Nú var eigi sein at konungi til mótsins, því at hann kom í fyrsta lagi.	Now was not late to-come the-king to the-meeting, because that he came to first had.	Now the king was not late in coming to the meeting, because he had arrived first.
Var hann þá blíðligr í yfirbragði.	Was he then happily in complexion.	He was then happy in his complexion.
Hann stóð upp ok mælti:	He stood up and spoke:	He stood up and spoke:
"Nú eru góð tíðendi at segja.	"Now there-are good tidings to say.	"Now there is good news to say.
Þat er ekki nema upplost ok lygi, er þér heyrðuð sagt um ófriðinn fyrra dag.	That is not except false-rumour and lie, that you heard said about un-peace the-first day.	That was nothing except a false rumour and a lie that you heard said about war the other day.
Viljum vér nú leyfa hverju skipi ór landi at fara þangat, sem hverr vill sínu skipi halda.	Wish we now allow each ship out-of lands to travel from-there, as each wishes their ship to-hold.	We now wish to allow each ship out of our lands to travel where they wish with their ships.
Komið aftr at hausti ok færið oss gersimar.	Come back in the-autumn and bring us treasures.	Come back in the autumn, and bring us treasures.
En þér skuluð hafa af oss í mót gæði ok vingan".	But you should have from us in return good-things and friendship".	Then you shall have good things and friendship in return from us".
Allir kaupmenn, er þar váru, urðu þessu fegnir ok báðu hann tala konunga heilstan.	All the-traders, who there were, became this celebrated and bid him speak the-king thanks.	All the traders who were there celebrated at this and spoke thanks to the king.
Fór Halldórr til Íslands um sumarit ok var þann vetr með frændum sínum.	Travelled Halldor to Iceland about summer and was then winter with father his.	Halldor travelled to Iceland around summer and was there with his father for the winter.

The Tale of Halldor Snorrason II (Old Norse)

Old Norse	Literal	English
Hann fór útan eftir um sumarit ok þá enn til hirðar Haralds konungs, ok er svá sagt at Halldórr var þá eigi jafnfylginn konungi sem fyrr, ok sat hann eftir um aftna, þá er konungr gekk at sofa.	He travelled out after about summer and then was to court Harald the-king, and was so said that Halldor was then not equally-following the-king as before, and sat he after about evening, then when the-king went to sleep.	He travelled around summer and was then in the court of king Harald, and so it was said that Halldor was not the same follower of the king that he was before, and he sat up in the evening after the king had gone to sleep.

2

Maðr hét Þórir Englandsfari ok hafði verit inn mesti kaupmaðr ok lengi í siglingum til ýmissa landa ok fært konungi gersimar.	A-man named Thorir England-Traveller and had been the most trading-man and long with sailing to various lands and bringing the-king treasure.	A man was named Thorir the England-Traveller, and he had been the greatest trader and had long sailed to various lands to bring the king treasure.
Þórir var hirðmaðr Haralds konungs ok þá mjök gamall.	Thorir was court-man Harald the-king and then much old.	Thorir was a court man of king Harald and was then very old.
Þórir kom at máli við konung ok mælti:	Thorir came to speak with the-king and spoke:	Thorir came to speak with the king and said:
"Ek er maðr gamall, sem þér vitið, ok mæðumst ek mjök.	"I am a-man old, as you know, and tired I-am much.	"I am an old man as you know, and I am very tired.
Þykkjumst ek nú eigi til færr at fylgja hirðsiðum, minni at drekka eða um aðra hluti, þá sem til heyra.	Think I now not to travel to follow king's-men-customs, mine to drink or about other things, then as to hear.	I now do not think I can follow the customs of the king's men, less drinking or other things which are heard of.
Mun nú annars leita verða, þótt þetta sé bezt ok blíðast, at vera með yðr".	Should now another seek to-be, though it is best and happiest, to be with you".	I should now seek another place to be, though it is best and happiest to be with you".
Konungr svarar:	The-king answered:	The king answered:
"Þar er okkr hægt til órráða, vinr.	"There is our possible to solution, friend.	"There is a possible solution, friend".
Ver með hirðinni ok drekk ekki meira en þú vill, í mínu leyfi".	Be with court and drink not more than you wish, with my leave".	Be with the court and do not drink more than you wish, with my leave".
Bárðr hét maðr upplenzkr, góðr drengr ok ekki gamall.	Bard was-named a-man an-Upplander, good fellow and not old.	There was a man named Bard, an Upplander, a good fellow and not old.

The Tale of Halldor Snorrason II (Old Norse)

Old Norse	Literal	English
Hann var með Haraldi konungi í miklum kærleikum.	He was with Harald the-king in much dearly-loved.	He was with king Harald and much loved by him.
Váru þeir sessunautar, Bárðr, Þórir ok Halldórr.	Were they sitting-together, Bard, Thorir and Halldor.	They were sitting together, Bard, Thorir, and Halldor.
Ok eitt kveld, er konungr gekk þar fyrir, er þeir sátu ok drukku, í því bili gaf Halldórr upp hornit.	And one evening, when the-king went there before, were they sat and drinking, in that moment gave Halldor up the-drinking-horn.	And one evening when the king went before where they sat drinking, in that moment Halldor gave up the drinking horn.
Þat var dýrshorn mikit ok skyggt vel.	It was stag-horn huge and shaded well.	It was a stag horn, and very transparent.
Sá gerla í gegnum, at hann hafði drukkit vel til hálfs við Þóri.	So completely in through, that he had drunk well to half against Thorir.	So completely through, that it could be seen that he had drunk more than half compared to Thorir
En honum gekk seint af at drekka.	Who he went slowly of to drink.	who drank slowly.
Þá mælti konungr:	Then spoke the-king:	Then the king spoke:
"Seint er þó menn at reyna, Halldórr",	"Slow it-is though people to know, Halldor",	"It is slow to get to know Halldor",
segir hann,	said he,	he said,
"er þú níðist á drykkju við gamalmenni ok hleypr at vændiskonum um síðkveldum, en fylgir eigi konungi þínum".	"that you down the drinks against old-men and run to prostitutes about late-evening, while following not king yours".	"that you down the drinks against old men, and run to prostitutes late in the evening, while not following your king".
Halldórr svarar engu, en Bárðr fann, at honum mislíkaði umræða ksonungs.	Halldor answered none, but Bard found, that he misliked discussion the-king's.	Halldor did not answer, but Bard found that he disliked the king's words.
Fór Bárðr þegar um myrgininn snemma á fund konungs.	Went Bard straight-away about morning early to find the-king.	Bard went straight away early in the morning to find the king.
"Þó ert þú nú árrisull, Bárðr",	"Though are you now early-riser, Bard",	"Though you are an early riser, Bard",
segir konungr.	said the-king.	said the king.
"Em ek nú kominn",	"Am I now come",	"And I have now come",

The Tale of Halldor Snorrason II (Old Norse)

Old Norse	Literal	English
kvað Bárðr,	said Bard,	said Bard,
"at ávíta yðr, herra.	"to warn you, lord.	"to warn you lord.
Þér mæltuð illa ok ómakliga í gærkveld til Halldórs, vinar yðvars, er þér kennduð honum, at hann drykki sleitiliga, því at þat var horn Þóris, ok hafði hann unnit ok ætlaði at bera til skapkers, ef eigi drykki Halldórr fyrir hann.	You spoke ill and undeservedly about last-night to Halldor, friend yours, when you taught him, that he drank unfairly, because that it was horn Thorir's, and had he deserved and intended to bear to large-vessel, if not drink Halldor before him.	You spoke badly and unfairly last night to Halldor, your friend, when you told him that he drank unfairly, because it was Thorir's horn, and he deserved and intended to bear a large vessel if Halldor was not drinking before him.
Þat er ok in mesta lygi, er þér mæltuð, at hann færi at léttlætiskonum, en kjósa myndi menn, at hann fylgði þér fastara".	It is also the most lie, that you spoke, that he went to prostitutes, than choose should people, to him follow you more-fixedly".	It is also the greatest lie that you said he went to prostitutes, although people would rather that he followed you more closely".
Konungr svarar ok lét, at þeir myndi semja þetta mál með sér, þá er þeir Halldórr fyndist.	The-king answered and had, that they would negotiate this matter with him, then when they Halldor found.	The king answered that he would negotiate this matter with him when he met Halldor next.
Hittir Bárðr Halldór ok segir honum góð orð konungs til hans ok kvað einsætt vera, at hann léti sér einskis þykkja um vert orðaframkast konungs, ok á Bárðr inn bezta hlut at með þeim.	Found Bard Halldor and said he good words the-king's to him and said clearly being, that he let himself nothing think about worthy outburst the-king's, and this Bard the best part that between them.	Bard found Halldor and told him the king's good words, and that he should let himself think no worth of the king's outburst, and this is how Bard tried to put the best part between them.
Líðr fram at jólum, ok er heldr fátt um með þeim konungi ok Halldóri.	Passed from to Yule, and was rather few about with them the-king and Halldor.	Time passed until Yule, and there was little between the king and Halldor.
Ok er at jólum kemr, þá eru víti upp sögð, sem þar er tízka til.	And when that Yule came, then they-were signalled up told, as there was custom to.	And when Yule came, were they signalled up as was the custom.
Ok einn morgun jólanna er breytt hringingum.	And one morning Yule was changed bell-ringing.	And one morning during Yule, the bell ringing was changed.

The Tale of Halldor Snorrason II (Old Norse)

Old Norse	Literal	English
Gáfu kertisveinar klokkurum fé til at hringja miklu fyrr en vant var, ok varð Halldórr víttr ok fjölði annarra manna, ok settust í hálm um daginn ok skyldu drekka vítin.	Gave court-men clocks payment for to ring much before than expected was, and became Halldor reprimanded and many other people, and sat in the-straw about the-day and should drink penalty.	The court men gave the bell ringers payment to ring the bells much before it was expected, and Halldor was reprimanded along with many other people, who had to sit on the floor in the straw and drink from the penalty horn.
Halldórr sitr í rúmi sínu, ok færa þeir honum eigi at síðr vítit, en hann lézt eigi drekka myndu.	Halldor sat in seat his, and brought they him none the less the-penalty, and he had not drank would.	Halldor sat in his room, and they none the less brought him the penalty horn, and he would not drink from it.
Þeir segja þá konungi til.	They told then the-king about.	They told the king about it.
"Þat mun eigi satt",	"That could not be-true",	"That could not be true",
segir konungr, „ok mun hann við taka, ef ek færi honum",	said the-king, „and should he with take, if I bring him",	said the king,
- tekr síðan vítishornit ok gengr at Halldóri.	- took then penalty-horn and went to Halldor.	"and he should take it if I bring it to him", and he took the penalty horn and went to Halldor.
Hann stendr upp í móti honum.	He stood up in meeting him.	He stood up upon meeting him.
Konungr biðr hann drekka vítit.	The-king asked him to-drink the-penalty.	The king asked him to drink the penalty.
Halldórr svarar:	Halldor answered:	Halldor answered:
"Ek þykkjumst ekki víttr at heldr, þó at þér setið brögð til hringingar til þess eins at gera mönnum víti".	"I think not penalty to hold, though that you set a-trick to bell-ringing to this alone to do people punishment".	"I don't think to hold the penalty, though you set a trick to the bell ringing only to punish people".
Konungr svarar:	The-king answered:	The king answered:
"Þú munt drekka skulu vítit þó eigi síðr en aðrir menn".	"You must drink should penalty though not less than other people".	"You must drink the penalty no less than other people".
"Vera má þat, konungr",	"Be may that, king",	"That may be, king",
segir Halldórr,	said Halldor,	said Halldor,

The Tale of Halldor Snorrason II (Old Norse)

Old Norse	Literal	English
"at þú komir því á leið, at ek drekka,	"that you come with to pass, that I drink,	"that it shall come to pass that I drink.
en þat kann ek þó segja þér, at eigi myndi Sigurðr sýr fá nauðgat Snorra goða til",	but that know I though say to-you, that not would Sigurd Sow gave force Snorri the-priest to",	But I know to say to you that Sigurd Sow would not have forced Snorri the Priest to",
- ok vill seilast til hornsins, sem hann gerir, ok drekkr af, en konungr reiðist mjök ok gengr til rúms síns.	- and willed to-reach for the-horn, as he went, and drank of, as the-king commanded much and went to room his.	and he reached for the penalty horn, and drank as much as the king commanded, and went to his room.
Ok er kemr inn átti dagr jóla, var mönnum gefinn máli.	And when came the eighth day Yule, were people given payment.	And when the eighth day of Yule came, people were given payment.
Þat var kallat Haraldsslátta.	That was called Harald's-money.	That was called Harald's money.
Var meiri hlutr kopars, þat bezta kosti, at væri helmings silfr.	Was greater part copper, that best benefit, that had half silver.	It was for the greater part copper, and the best of it was half silver.
Ok er Halldórr tók málann, hefir hann í möttulsskauti sínu silfrit ok lítr á ok sýnist eigi skírt málasilfrit, lýstr undir neðan annarri hendi, ok ferr þat allt í hálm niðr.	And when Halldor took payment, had he in cloak-lap his the-silver and looked at and seemed not pure silverware, struck under below other hand, and went it all in straw below.	And when Halldor took the payment, he put the silver in the lap of his cloak, and it seemed not to be pure silver, he swept it down with his other hand and it all went onto the straw on the floor below.
Bárðr mælti, kvað hann illa með fara.	Bard spoke, said he badly with went.	Bard spoke, and said that he was behaving badly:
"Mun konungr þykkjast svívirðr í ok leitat á við hann um málagjöfna".	"Would the-king consider dishonourable of and consider to with him about payment".	"The king would consider this dishonourable, considering with him about payment".
"Ekki má nú fara at slíku",	"Not may now go that such",	"It may not go that way",
segir Halldórr,	said Halldor,	said Halldor,
"litlu hættir nú til".	"little way now to".	"there is little to be done now".

3

Nú er frá því sagt, at þeir búa skip sín eftir jólin.	Now was from of said, that they prepared ships theirs after Yule.	Now it was said that they prepared their ships after Yule.

The Tale of Halldor Snorrason II (Old Norse)

Old Norse	Literal	English
Ætlar konungr suðr fyrir land.	Intended the-king south along the-land.	The king intended to travel south along the land.
Ok er konungr var mjök svá búinn, þá bjóst Halldórr ekki, ok mælti Bárðr:	And when the-king was much so prepared, then readied Halldor not, and spoke Bard:	And when the king was so well prepared, Halldor did not prepare, and Bard said,
"Hví býstu eigi, Halldórr?"	"Why prepared not, Halldor?"	"Why do you not prepare Halldor?"
"Eigi vil ek",	"Not wish I",	"I do not want to,"
segir hann,	said he,	he said,
"ok ekki ætla ek at fara.	"and not intend I to travel.	"and I do not intend to travel.
Sé ek nú, at konungr þokkar ekki mitt mál".	See I now, that the-king favours not my measure".	I see now that the king does not like my case".
Bárðr segir:	Bard said:	Bard said:
"Hann mun þó at vísu vilja, at þú farir".	"He would though that certainly wish, that you travel".	"Though he will want you to travel".
Ferr Bárðr síðan ok hittir konung, segir honum, at Halldórr býst ekki.	Went Bard afterwards and found the-king, said he, that Halldor prepares not.	Afterwards Bad went and found the king, and he told him that Halldor had not prepared,
"Máttu svá ætla, at vandskipaðr mun þér vera stafninn í stað hans".	"May-you so suppose, that difficult would you be the-prow in replace his".	"you may suppose that it would be difficult to replace him in the prow of the ship".
Konungr mælti:	The-king spoke:	The king spoke:
"Seg honum, at ek ætla, at hann skyli mér fylgja, ok þetta er ekki alhugat, fæð sja, er með okkr er um hríð".	"Say to-him, that I intend, that he shall with-me follow, and this is not resolved, sadness see, that with us is about awhile".	"Tell him that I intend that he shall follow with me, and this is not resolved, this sadness that has been seen between us for a while".
Bárðr hittir Halldór ok lætr, at konungr vili enskis kostar láta hans þjónustu, ok þat ræðst ór, at Halldórr ferr, ok halda þeir konungr suðr með landi.	Bard found Halldor and leave, that the-king willed no choice losing his service, and that commanded from, that Halldor went, and held they the-king south along the-land.	Bard found Halldor and put to him that the king gave no choice to lose his service, and that it was a command, and from that Halldor went and they held with the king south along the land.

The Tale of Halldor Snorrason II (Old Norse)

Old Norse	Literal	English
Ok einhverja nótt, er þeir sigldu, þá mælti Halldórr til þess, er stýrði:	And one-such night, that they sailed, then spoke Halldor to that, who steered:	And on one such night the sailed, Halldor spoke to the steersman,
"Lát ýkva",	"Let-it veer",	"let it veer",
segir hann.	said he.	he said.
Konungr mælti til stýrimanns:	The-king spoke to the-steersman:	The king spoke to the steersman,
"Halt svá fram, segir hann.	"Hold so forwards, said he.	"hold straight on", he said.
Halldórr mælti öðru sinni:	Halldor spoke a-second his:	Halldor spoke a second time:
"Lát ýkva".	"Let-it veer".	"Let it veer".
Konungr segir enn á sömu leið.	The-king said then of the-same way.	The king said the same way.
Halldórr mælti:	Halldor spoke:	Halldor spoke:
"Beint stefnið þér skerit".	"Direction heading you-to a-rock".	"You are heading directly for a rock".
Ok at því varð þeim.	And that accordingly became of-them.	And so it happened of them.
Því næst gekk undan skipinu undirhlutinn, ok varð þá at flytja til lands með öðrum skipum, ok síðan var skotit landtjald ok bætt at skipinu.	Because next went under the-ship the-under-part, and became then that carried to land with other ships, and afterwards were launched land-tents and repaired the ship.	Because next the underneath of the ship went and it then had to be carried to the land with other ships, and then a land tent was set up, and they ship was repaired.
Við þat vaknar Bárðr, er Halldórr bindr húðfat sitt.	With that awoke Bard, that Halldor tied-up hammock his.	With that Bard awoke to find Halldor tying up his hammock.
Bárðr spyrr, hvat hann ætlast fyrir,	Bard asked, what he intended for,	Bard asked what his intention was.
en Halldórr kvaðst ætla á byrðing, er lá skammt frá þeim, -	then Halldor said intend to merchant-ship, that lay short-distance from them, -	Then Halldor said that he intended to go to a merchant ship that lay a short distance from them,

The Tale of Halldor Snorrason II (Old Norse)

Old Norse	Literal	English
"ok kann vera, at nú leggi sundr reyki vára, ok er þetta fullreynt.	"and can it-be, that now lay separate smoke going, and is that fully-tested.	"and it may be that now our smoke is falling apart, and it has been fully tried".
Ok eigi vil ek, at konungr spilli oftar skipum sínum eða öðrum gersimum mér til svívirðingar ok at mér beri þá verr en áðr".	And not wish I, the king spoil more-often ships his or other treasure me to disgrace and that me bear then worse than before".	And I do not want the king to spoil his ships or other treasures more often to disgrace me, and treat me then worse than before".
"Bíð enn",	"Wait still",	"Still, wait",
segir Bárðr,	said Bard,	said Bard,
"ek vil enn hitta konung.	"I will but find the-king.	"I will just find the king".
Ok er hann kemr, mælti konungr:	And when he came, spoke-to the-king:	And when he came the king spoke:
"Snemma ertu á fótum, Bárðr".	"Soon are-you about feed, Bard".	"You are early on your feet, Bard".
"Svá er nú þörf, herra.	"So is now needed, lord.	"So it is needed now, lord.
Halldórr er í brautbúnaði ok þykkir þú óvingjarnliga til sín gert hafa, ok er nökkut vant at gæta til með ykkr.	Halldor is to away-prepared and thinks you unfriendly to him done have, and is something difficult that take-care to with you-two.	Halldor is preparing to go away and thinks that you have been unfriendly towards him, and it's difficult to keep the peace between you two.
Ætlar hann nú í brott ok ráðast til skips ok fara út til Íslands með reiði, ok ferr þá ómakliga ykkarr skilnaðr,	Intends he now to away and appoint to a-ship and travel out to Iceland with anger, and goes then undeservedly with-you parting,	He now intends to go away and join a ship and travel to Iceland in anger, and that's not a proper way for you to part.
ok þat hygg ek, at varla fáir þú þér annan mann jafntraustan honum".	and it think I, that hardly few you to-you another man equally-trustworthy as-him".	And I think that you will hardly find another man as equally trustworthy as him".
Konungr lét, at þeir myndi enn sættast, ok kvað sér ekki myndu at þessu þykkja.	The-king had, it they would still reconcile, and said himself not would of this think.	The king said that they would still reconcile and said he would not think about it.
Bárðr hittir Halldór ok segir honum vingjarnlig orð konungs.	Bard found Halldor and told him friendly words the-king's.	Bard found Halldor and told him the king's friendly words.
Halldórr svarar:	Halldor answered:	Halldor answered:

The Tale of Halldor Snorrason II (Old Norse)

Old Norse	Literal	English
"Til hvers skal ek honum þjóna lengr, þatki at ek fá mála minn falslaust?"	"To how shall I him serve longer, that-not that I get matter mine without-fraud?"	"Why should I serve him any longer? Let me have my case without fraud".
Bárðr mælti:	Bard spoke:	Bard said,
"Get eigi þess.	"Get not like-this.	"Don't talk like this.
Vel máttu þér þat líka láta, er lendra manna synir hafa, ok ekki fórtu at því með vægð næsta sinni, er þú slótt niðr í hálm silfrinu ok ónýttir,	Well may you that like allow, what is-paid people sons have, and not went-you that therefore with grace next-to yourself, when you struck down into the-straw the-silver and un-used,	Well, you might as well have what the sons of the land have, and you did not do it mercifully the next time you struck the silver down in the straw and wasted it.
ok máttu víst vita, at konungi þykki þat sviviðliga til sín gert".	and may certainly know, that the-king thought that dishonourable to him done".	And you must know that the king considers it disgraceful to do so".
Halldórr svarar:	Halldor answered:	Halldor answered:
"Eigi má ek þat vita, at neitt sinn hafi jafnmjök logizt í um fylgðina mína sem í málagjöfna konungs".	"Not may I that certainly, that nothing he has equally-much cheated in about following mine as in payment the-king's".	"I do not know of having cheated him in my following as much as he has cheated me with the king's payment".
"Satt mun þat vera",	"True would that be",	"That may be true",
segir Bárðr,	said Bard,	said Bard,
"biðleika, enn vil ek hitta konung".	"wait then will I find the-king".	"wait, then I will find the king".
Ok svá gerði hann.	And so did he.	And he did so.
Ok er Bárðr hitti konung, mælti hann:	And when Bard found the-king, spoke he:	And when Bard found the king, he spoke:
"Fá Halldóri mála sinn skíran, því at verðr er hann at hafa".	"Get Halldor payment his cleared, because that worth is he to have".	"Get Halldor his payment cleared, because he is worth having".
Konungr svarar:	The-king answered:	The king answered:

The Tale of Halldor Snorrason II (Old Norse)

Old Norse	Literal	English
"Lízt þér eigi nökkur svá djörfung í at krefja Halldóri annars mála en taka lendra manna synir, með slíkri svívirðing sem hann fór með málanum næstum?"	"Appears to-you not something so bold that to demand Halldor another payment than take payment people's sons, And with such disgrace as he did with payment before?"	"Does it not appear you you somewhat bold to demand Halldor a payment other than people's sons, and with such disgrace as he did with his last payment?"
Bárðr svarar:	Bard answered:	Bard answered:
"Á hitt er at líta, herra, er miklu er meira vert, drengskap hans ok vináttu ykkra, er lengi hefir góð verit, ok þar með stórmennsku þína,	"To find that to look, lord, that much is more worth, honour his and friendship yours, that long has good been, and there with greatness yours,	"The other thing is to look, lord, at who is much more valuable, his boyhood and your friendship that has been good for a long time and thus your greatness.
ok veiztu skap Halldórs ok stirðlæti, ok er þat þinn vegr at gera honum sóma".	and know-you mood Halldor's and hard-temper, and that it your way that to-do him honour".	And we know Halldór's mood and stiffness, and it's your way to do him honor".
Konungr mælti:	The-king spoke:	The king said:
"Fái honum silfrit".	"Give him the-silver".	"Give him the silver".
Var nú svá gert.	Was now so done.	Now this was done.
Kemr Bárðr til Halldórs ok færir honum tólf aura brennda ok mælti:	Came Bard to Halldor and brought him twelve ounces burnt and spoke:	Bard came to Halldor and brought him twelve ounces of refined silver and spoke:
"Sér þú eigi, at þú hefir slíkt, er þú brekar af konungi, ok hann vill, at þú hafir slíkt af honum, sem þú þykkist þurfa".	"See you not, that you have such, that you keep-asking of the-king, and he wishes, that you have such of him, as you think you-need".	"Do you not see that you ask of the king, and he wishes to to have what you think you need, if only you ask for it?"
Halldórr svarar:	Halldor answered:	Halldor answeed:
"Eigi skal ek þó oftar vera á konungsskipinu, ok ef hann vill hafa mitt föruneyti lengr, þá vil ek hafa skip til stjórnar ok eignast þat".	"Not shall I though frequent be in the-king's-ship, and if he wishes to-have my companionship longer, then wish I to-have ship to steer and own it".	"I shall not be on the king's ship more often, and if he wishes to have me in his company any longer, then I wish to have my own ship to steer".
Bárðr svarar:	Bard answered:	Bard answered:

The Tale of Halldor Snorrason II (Old Norse)

Old Norse	Literal	English
"Þat samir eigi, at lendir menn láti skip sín fyrir þér, ok ertu of framgjarn".	"It so not, to landed men have ships theirs for you, and are-you over ambitious".	"It is not so that landed man give up their ships for you, and you are over-ambitious".
Halldórr kvaðst eigi fara myndu elligar.	Halldor said not travelling would otherwise.	Halldor said that he would not travel otherwise.
Bárðr segir konungi, hvers beitt er af Halldórs hendi, -	Bard told the-king, what asked had of Halldor's hand, -	Bard told the king what Halldor had asked for
"ok ef hásetar þess skips eru jafntraustir sem stýrimaðr, þá mun vel hlýða".	"and if sailors these ships were equally-trustworthy as steersman, then would well listen-to".	"and if the sailors of these ships were equally trustworthy as the steersman then they would listen to him well".
Konungr mælti:	The-king spoke:	The king said,
"Þótt þetta þykki framarla mælt vera, þá skal þó af nökkut gera".	"Though this think forward spoken is, then shall though of something do".	"Though this be thought to be far-fetched, something must be done".
Sveinn ór Lyrgju, lendr maðr, stýrði skipi.	Fellow from Lyrgja, land man, steered a-ship.	Svein from Lyrgja, a landed man, steered a ship.
Konungr lét hann kalla á mál við sik.	The-king had him called and conversed with him.	The king had him called and discussed with him.
"Þannug er farit",	"That-way is travelled",	"It is so",
segir konungr,	said the-king,	said the king,
"sem þú veizt, at þú ert maðr stórættaðr.	"that you know, that you are a-man of-high-family.	"that you know that you are a man of great family.
Vil ek fyrir því, at þú sér á mínu skipi, en ek mun þar fá annan mann til skipstjórnar.	Wish I for therefore, that you be on my ship, but I should there get another man to ship-steer.	I want you to be on my ship, but I will get another man to captain it.
Þú ert maðr vizkr, ok vil ek einkum hafa þik við ráð mín".	You are a-man wise, and wish I especially have you with advise me".	You are a man of wisdom and I especially want you with my advice".
Hann segir:	He said:	He said:
"Meir hefir þú aðra menn haft við þínar ráðagerðir hér til, ok til þess em ek litt færr, eða hverjum er þá skipit ætlat?"	"More have you other men had with you advice-giving here to, and to this am I little accomplished, but who is then ship intended?"	"You have had other men with your advice so far and to the point that I can do little, but who is the ship intended for?"

The Tale of Halldor Snorrason II (Old Norse)

Old Norse	Literal	English
"Halldórr Snorrason skal hafa",	"Halldor Snorrason shall have",	"Halldor Snorrason shall have it",
segir konungr.	said the-king.	said the king.
Sveinn segir:	The-fellow said:	Sveinn said:
"Eigi kom mér þat í hug, at þú myndir íslenzkan mann láta taka af mér skipstjórn".	"Not came to-me that to think, that you would Icelander man have take from me ship-steering".	"It never occurred to me that you would choose an Icelander for that, still take me from the captaincy".
Konungr mælti:	The-king spoke:	The king said,
"Hans ætt er eigi verri á Íslandi en þín hér í Nóregi, ok eigi hefir enn alllangt síðan liðit, er þeir váru norrænir, er nú byggja Ísland".	"His ancestry is not worse as Icelander but your forces in Norway, and not has-been but all-long since passed, that they were Norwegians, that now settle Iceland".	"His family is no worse in Iceland than yours here in Norway, and it has not been long since they were Norwegians who now inhabit Iceland".
Nú ferr þat fram, sem konungr vill, at Halldórr tekr við skipi, ok fóru síðan austr til Óslo, tóku þar veizlur.	Now went that from, as the-king wished, that Halldor took with ship, and travelled afterwards east to Oslo, took there feasts.	Now it went as the king wished, that Halldor took the ship, and travelled afterwards east to Oslo, where they took to feasting.

4

Þat er sagt, einnhvern dag, er þeir konungr sátu við drykkju, ok var Halldórr þar í konungs stofunni, at sveinar hans kómu þar, þeir er skipit skyldu varðveita, ok váru allir vátir ok sögðu, at þeir Sveinn höfðu tekit skipit, en rekit þá á kaf.	It was said, one-such day, that there the-king sat with drinking, and was Halldor there in the-king's chamber, the fellows his came there, they were ship should guard-over, and were all wet and said, that they Svein had taken the-ship, and thrown them to overboard.	It was said that one day the king and Halldor sat drinking in the king's chambers, and in came the men who were watching over his ship came in, and they were all wet, and they said that Svein had taken the ship and thrown them overboard.
Halldórr stóð upp ok gekk fyrir konung ok spurði, hvárt hann skyldi eiga skipit ok haldast þat, er konungr hafði mælt.	Halldor stood up and went before the-king and asked, how he should own the-ship and hold that, which the-king had spoken-of.	Halldor stood up and went before the king and asked whether he would own the ship as the king had promised.

The Tale of Halldor Snorrason II (Old Norse)

Old Norse	Literal	English
Konungr svarar ok kvað þat at vísu haldast skyldu, kvaddi síðan hirðina, at þeir skyldi taka sex skip ok fara með Halldóri ok hafa þrenna skipun á hverju.	The-king answered and said that it certainly hold should, called since guardsmen, that they should take six ships and travel with Halldor and have treble crew on each.	The king answered and said that he would keep his promise, and then called to the guardsmen that they should take six ships, travelling with a treble crew on each.
Þeir snúa nú eftir þeim Sveini, ok lætr hann eltast at landi, ok þegar hljóp Sveinn á land upp, en þeir Halldórr tóku skipit ok fóru til konungs.	They turned now after they Svein, and let he chased to land, and there ran Svein on-the land up, and there Halldor took the-ship and went to the-king.	They now turned after Svein and gave him chase ashore, and there Svein ran ashore, but Halldor took the ship and went to the king.
Ok er veizlum var lokit, ferr konungr norðr með landi ok til Þrándheims, er á líðr sumarit.	And when the-feasts were ended, went the-king north along the-land and to Trondheim, where then passed summer.	And when the feasts were over, the king went north along the land, and to Trondheim, when the summer had passed.
Sveinn ór Lyrgju sendi orð konungi, at hann vill gefa upp allt mál um skipit ok leggja á konungs vald, at hann skipi með þeim Halldóri, sem hann vill, ok vildi þó helzt kaupa skipit, ef konungi líkaði.	Svein from Lyrgja sent word to-the-king, that he wished to-give up all matter about the-ship and grant to-the-king power, that he ship with them Halldor, as he wished, and wished though rather purchase the-ship, if the-king liked.	Svein of Lyrgja sent word to the king that he wished to give up the whole matter and put it in the king's power, that the ship would be with Halldor as he wished, but would prefer to purchase the ship if it was to the king's liking.
Ok nú er konungr sér þat, at Sveinn skýtr öllu máli undir hans dóm, þá vill hann nú svá til bregða, er báðum mætti líka, falar skipit at Halldóri ok vill, at hann hafi verð sæmiligt, en Sveinn hafi skip, ok kaupir konungr skip, ok á Halldórr við hann um verð, ok gelzt allt upp, nema hálf mörk gulls stendr eftir.	And now as the-king saw that, of Svein launched all matter under his deeming, then wished he now so to foreclose, that both may like, bargain ship that Halldor and wished, that he had worth the-same, that Svein had ship, and bought the-king the-ship, and that Halldor with him about worth, and paid all up, except half a-mark gold stood behind.	And now the king saw that Svein gave the whole matter up to his judgement, that he now wished to settle the matter to the liking of both parties. The ship was purchased from Halldor and he wished that he had a price the same worth as Svein to have the ship, and the king bought the ship from Halldor, and with him was the price and gold all paid except for half a gold mark left behind.
Heimtir Halldórr lítt, enda galzt þat ekki, ok ferr svá fram um vetrinn.	Got Halldor little, end payment that not, and went so forward about winter.	Halldor did not demand the closure of the payment, and so things went on over the winter.

The Tale of Halldor Snorrason II (Old Norse)

Old Norse	Literal	English
Ok er vára tók, segir Halldórr konungi, at hann vill til Íslands um sumarit, ok kvað sér vel koma, at þá gyldist þat, sem eftir var kaupverðsins.	And as spring took, said Halldor to-the-king, that he wished to Iceland about summer, and said he well come, that then repay that, which remained was ship's-worth.	And as spring came, Halldor said to the king that he wished to travel to Iceland in the summer, and it would be well if he could repay the remainder of the ship's worth.
En konungr ferr heldr undan um gjaldit ok þykkir ekki betr, er hann heimtir, en ekki bannar hann Halldóri útferð, ok býr hann skip sitt um várit í ánni Nið ok leggr út síðan við Bröttueyri.	But the-king went rather from-under about the-payment and seemed not better, that he got, then not ban him Halldor out-travelling, and prepared he ship his about spring in the-river Nid and laid out afterwards with Bratteyar.	But the king escaped the payment, and thought not better that he demanded, but did not ban Halldor from travelling, and he prepared his ship around spring in the river Nid, nd laid out afterwards at Bratteyar.
Ok er þeir váru albúnir ok byrvænligt var, þá gengr Halldórr upp í bæinn með nökkura menn síð um aftan.	And when they were all-prepared and promising-wind were, then going Halldor up out-of town with some men later about evening.	And then they were all prepared and with a promising wind, then Halldor went up in the town with some men later in the evening.
Hann var með vápnum,	He was with weapons,	He was armed with weapons.
gengu þar til, er þau konungr ok dróttning sváfu.	went they to, where then the-king and the-queen slept.	They then went to where the king and queen slept.
Förunautar hans stóðu úti undir loftinu, en hann gengr inn með vápnum sínum, ok verðr glymr ok skark af honum, ok vakna þau konungr við, ok spyrr konungr, hverr brjótist at þeim um nætr.	Companions his stood outside under the-air, then he went inside with weapons his, and came echo and noise of him, and awoke then the-king with, and asked the-king, who breaking in-on them about night.	His companions stood outside, and he went inside and made a noise with his weapons which echoed and woke the king, who asked who was breaking in on them in the night.
"Hér er Halldórr kominn ok búinn til hafs, ok kominn á byrr, ok er nú ráð at gjalda fét".	"Here is Halldor come and prepared to sea, and coming is fair-wind, and is now the-matter to pay wealth".	"Halldor is here, prepared to go to sea, and a fair wind is coming, and now is the matter to settle the payment".
"Ekki má þat nú svá skjótt",	"Not may that now so swiftly",	"Now that may not be done so swiftly",
segir konungr,	said the-king,	said the king,
"ok munum vér greiða fé á morgun".	"and should we assist payment in the-morning".	"and we shall assist with the payment in the morning".

The Tale of Halldor Snorrason II (Old Norse)

Old Norse	Literal	English
"Nú vil ek þegar hafa",	"Now wish I straightaway have",	"Now I wish to have it straight away",
segir Halldórr,	said Halldor,	said Halldor,
"ok munkat ek nú erendlaust fara.	"and shall I now errand-without go.	"and I shall not go without it.
Kann ek ok skap þitt, ok veit ek, hversu þér mun líka þessi för mín ok fjárheimta, hvégi sem þú lætr nú.	Know I also mood yours, and know I, how-so you shall like this going mine and money-insisting, which as you behave now.	I also know your mood, and I know how you would like me to go, and am demanding the money which you will leave now.
Mun ek lítt trúa þér heðan frá, enda er ósýnt, at vit finnimst svá vilgis oft, at mitt sé vænna, ok skal nú neyta þess, ok sé ek, at dróttning hefir hring á hendi því hófi mikinn.	Shall I little believe you hence from, conclude as unseen, that with found so very often, that mine so expected, and shall now use this, and see I, that the-queen has a-ring on hand therefore modest greatly.	I shall not trust you again from now on, it is not clear how often we find that I have the advantage, so I shall now take advantage of this, and I see that the queen has a ring on her hand, which is accordingly greatly modest.
Fá mér þann".	Give me it".	Give it to me".
Konungr svarar:	The-king answered:	The king answered:
"Þá verðum vit fara eftir skálum ok vega hringinn".	"Then worth with going after bowl and weigh the-ring".	"Then it is worth going after the bowls and weighing the ring".
"Ekki þarf þess",	"Not needed is-this",	"That is not needed",
segir Halldórr,	said Halldor,	said Halldor,
"tek ek hann fyrir hlut minn, enda muntu nú ekki prettum við koma at sinni, ok sel fram títt".	"take I it for share mine, and should now not trick with coming this time, and flip forward immediately".	"I will take it for my share, and you shall not try and trick me this time, and give it forward immediately".
Dróttning mælti:	The-queen spoke:	The queen spoke:
"Fá honum hringinn, sem hann beiðir.	"Give him the-ring, as he asks".	"Give him the ring, as he asks".
"Sér þú eigi",	"See you not",	"Do you not see",
segir hon,	said she,	she said,

The Tale of Halldor Snorrason II (Old Norse)

Old Norse	Literal	English
"at hann stendr yfir þér uppi með víghug?" -	"that he stands over you up with killing-mind?" -	"that he stands over you with a mind to kill?"
tekr síðan hringinn ok fær Halldóri.	took then the-ring and brought Halldor.	She then took the ring and brought it to Halldor.
Hann tekr við ok þakkar þeim báðum gjaldit ok biðr þau vel lifa, -	He took with and thanked them both payment and bid them well life, -	He took it and thanked them both for the payment and bid them a good life
"ok munum vér nú skilja",	"and shall we now separate",	"and we shall now separate".
-gengr nú út ok mælti við förunauta sína, biðr þá hlaupa sem tíðast til skipsins, -	-went now out and spoke with companions his, asked them to-run as swiftly to ship, -	He now went out and spoke with his companions, asking them to run swiftly to the ship
"því at ófúss em ek at dveljast lengi í bænum".	"because that unwilling am I to stay long in this-town".	because I am not willing to stay long in this town.
Þeir gera svá, koma á skipit, ok þegar vinda sumir upp segl, sumir eru at báti, sumir heimta upp ákkeri, ok bergst hverr, sem má.	They did so, came to the-ship, and straightaway wind some upped the-sails, some were at the-tow-boat, some drew up the-anchor, and best each, as may.	They did so, and came to the ship and straight away wind came and they upped the sails, some were at the tow boat, and some drew up the anchor, each doing the best they could.
Ok er þeir sigldu út, skorti eigi hornblástr í bænum, ok þat sá þeir síðast, at þrjú langskip váru á floti ok lögðu eftir þeim, en þó berr þá undan ok í haf.	And when they sailed out, shortly one horn-blast from the-city, and this saw they the-last, that three longships were in floating and laid after them, but though carried then under and to sea.	And shortly after they had sailed out, there was a horn blast from the city, and the last thing they saw were three longships floating and laid after them, though then they were carried out to sea.
Skilr þar með þeim, ok byrjaði Halldóri vel út til Íslands, en konungsmenn hurfu aftr, er þeir sá, er Halldór bar undan ok í haf út.	Separated there with them, and began Halldor well out to Iceland, but the-kings-men disappeared after, when they saw, that Halldor bore away-from and to sea out-of.	They separated with them there and Halldor started well out to Iceland, but the king's men turned bak when they saw that Halldor was carried away out to sea.

5

Halldórr Snorrason var mikill maðr vexti ok fríðr sýnum, allra manna styrkastr ok vápndjarfastr.	Halldor Snorrason was a-great man well-built and handsome in-appearance, of-all men strongest and weapons-bold.	Halldor Snorrason was a great man, well built, and handsome in appearance, the strongest of all men, and the best with weapons.

The Tale of Halldor Snorrason II (Old Norse)

Old Norse	Literal	English
Þat vitni bar Haraldr konungr Halldóri, at hann hefði verit með honum allra manna svá, at sízt brygði við váveifliga hluti, hvárt sem at höndum bar mannháska eða fagnaðartíðendi, þá var hann hvárki at glaðari né óglaðari.	That testimony gave Harald the-king Halldor, that he had been with him all men so, that least reacted with unexpected part, which was at hand bringing human-danger or good-news, then was he neither to gladness nor un-gladness.	King Harald gave a testimony of Halldor that of all the men he had been with, that he reacted least to an unexpected lot, which with hand carried danger or good news, he was neither happy nor unhappy.
Eigi neytti hann matar eða drakk eða svaf meira né minna en vanði hans var til, hvárt sem hann mætti blíðu eða stríðu.	Not consumed he food or drank or slept more nor less than custom his was to, each as he might joyful or stressful.	He did not eat or drink or sleep more not less than his custom, whether he was happy or stressful.
Halldórr var maðr fámæltr, stuttorðr, bermæltr, stygglyndr ok ómjúkr, kappgjarn í öllum hlutum, við hvern sem hann átti um.	Halldor was a-man of-few-words, short-worded, outspoken, quick-tempered and un-bending, self-willed in all things, against which as he had about.	Halldor was a man of few words, short, outspoken, quick tempered and ungiving, self-willed about everything that he had.
En þat kom illa við Harald konung, er hann hafði nóga aðra þjónustumenn.	But this came ill with Harald the-king, as he had enough other servants.	But this came badly against king Harald as he had enough other servants.
Kómu þeir því lítt lyndi saman, síðan Haraldr varð konungr í Nóregi.	Came they therefore little temper together, since Harald was king of Norway.	They did not get along well since Haraldur became king of Norway.
En er Halldórr kom til Íslands, gerði hann bú í Hjarðarholti.	But when Halldor came to Iceland, did he settle at Hjardarholt.	But when Halldór came to Iceland he made an estate in Hjarðarholt.
Nökkurum sumrum síðar sendi Haraldr konungr orð Halldóri Snorrasyni, at hann skyldi ráðast enn til hans, ok lét, at eigi skyldi verit hafa hans virðing meiri en þá, ef hann vildi farit hafa, ok engan mann skyldi hann hæra setja í Nóregi ótiginn, ef hann vildi þetta boð þekkjast.	Some summers later sent Harald the-king word-to Halldor Snorrason, that he should arrange then to him, and had, that not should be having his honour more than then, if he willed travel to-sea, and only man should he highest sit in Norway un-high-born, if he wished this invitation accept.	A few summers later, King Harald sent word to Halldor Snorrason that he should appoint him again, and put that his respect would not be greater than that if he wished to travel to sea, and that no man should sit higher than him in Norway if he wished to accept this invitation.
Halldórr svarar svá, er honum kómu þessi orð:	Halldor answered so, as to-him came these words:	Halldor answered when these words came to him:
"Ekki mun ek fara á fund Haralds konungs heðan af.	"Not should I travel to meet Harald the-king from-here of.	"I will not go to King Harald from now on.

The Tale of Halldor Snorrason II (Old Norse)

Old Norse	Literal	English
Mun nú hafa hvárr okkar þat, sem fengit hefir.	Should now have each ours that, which got we-have.	Each of us will now have what he has received.
Mér er kunnigt skaplyndi hans.	To-me it-is known mood-temper his.	His mood is known to me.
Veit ek gerla, at hann myndi þat efna, sem hann hét, at setja engan mann hæra í Noregi en mik, ef ek kæma á hans fund, því at hann myndi mik láta festa á inn hæsta gálga ef hann mætti ráða".	Know I completely, that he should that carry-out, which he promised, to sit no man higher in Norway but me, if I come to him to-meet, therefore that he should me have fasten to the highest gallows if he might prevail".	I know very well that he would do what he promised to put no man higher in Norway than me if I came to meet him, for he would have me fastened to the highest gallows if he could rule it".
Ok er á leið mjök ævi Haralds konungs, þá er sagt, at hann sendi Halldóri orð til, at hann skyldi senda honum melrakkabelgi, vildi gera láta af þeim yfir rekkju sína, því at konungr þóttist þurfa hlýs.	And when had passed much age Harald the-king, then that is-said, that he sent Halldor word to, that he should send him arctic-fox-furs, wished get have of them over bed his, because that the-king thought needed warmth.	And when king Harald became much passed with age, it is said that he sent word to Halldor that he should send him arctic fox furs, he wanted to let them go over his bed because the king thought he needed warmth.
Ok er Halldóri kom sjá orðsending konungs, þá er sagt, at hann skyti því orði við í fyrstu:	And as Halldor came so word-sending the-king, then was said, that he shot accordingly word against at first:	And when Halldor came to see the king's message, it is said that he replied first:
"Eldist árgalinn nú",	"Old-is the-cockerel now",	"The yearling is getting old now",
sagði hann, en sendi honum belgi.	said he, but sent him furs.	he said, but sent him arctic fox furs.
En ekki fundust þeir sjálfir, síðan er þeir skilðust í Þrándheimi, þó at þá yrði nökkut með stytti því sinni.	But not met they themselves, afterwards that the separated at Trondheim, though that then became somewhat with short of themselves.	But they did not meet each other since they had separated at Trondheim, though they had taken short leave with each other.
Bjó hann í Hjarðarholti til elli ok varð maðr gamall.	Farmed he in Hjardarholt until old-age and became a-man old.	He lived in Hjarðarholt until old age and became an old man.

Word List *(Old Norse to English)*

Old Norse	English
A, a	
aðra	other
aðrir	other
af	from, from, of, of
aftan	evening
aftna	evening
aftr	after, back
aga	turbulence
albúnir	all-prepared
alhugat	resolved
allir	all, all
alllangt	all-long
allra	all, of-all
allt	all, all
annan	another, another, the-next
annarra	other
annarri	other
annars	another
at	at, in, in-on, it, of, that, the, this, to, to-come
atgang	access
aura	ounces
austan	east
austr	east
Á, á	
á	about, and, as, at, had, in, is, of, on, on-the, that, the, then, this, to
áðr	before, other
áhöfnina	crew
áhyggjusvip	worried-face
ákalsi	calling
ákkeri	the-anchor
álaga	stress
ánni	the-river
árgalinn	the-cockerel
árrisull	early-riser
átti	eighth, had
ávíta	warn
Æ, æ	
ætla	intend, suppose
ætlaði	intended
ætlar	intended, intends
ætlast	intended
ætlat	intended
ætt	ancestry
ævi	age
B, b	
báðu	bid
báðum	both
bæði	both
bæinn	town
bæjarmenn	townspeople
bænum	the-city, the-town, this-town
bætt	repaired
bann	a-ban
bannar	ban
bar	bore, bringing, gave
Bárðr	Bard (name)
báti	the-tow-boat
beiða	asked
beiðir	asks
beint	direction
beitt	asked
belgi	furs
bera	bear
bergst	best
beri	bear
bermæltr	outspoken
berr	bears, carried
betr	better
betra	better

Word List (Old Norse to English)

Old Norse	English
bezt	best
bezta	best
bíð	wait
bíða	wait
biðleika,	wait
biðr	asked, bid
bili	moment
bindr	tied-up
bjó	farmed, settled
bjóst	readied
bjuggu	preparations
blásit	trumpet-blown
blíðast	happiest
blíðligr	happily
blíðu	joyful
boð	invitation
brautbúnaði	away-prepared
bregða	foreclose
brekar	keep-asking
brennda	burnt
breytt	changed
brjótist	breaking
brögð	a-trick
brotin	violated
brott	away
Bröttueyri	Bratteyar (place)
brygði	reacted
bú	settle
búa	prepared
búinn	prepared
búit	prepared
búnaðinn	preparations
byggja	settle
býr	prepared
byrðing	merchant-ship
byrjaði	began
byrr	fair-wind
byrvænligt	promising-wind
býst	prepares
býstu	prepared

D, d

Old Norse	English
dag	day
daginn	the-day
dagr	day
danaher	Danish-forces
danakonungr	king-of-Denmark
Danmerkr	Denmark (place)
djörfung	bold
dögum	days
dóm	deeming
drakk	drank
drekk	drink
drekka	drank, drink, to-drink
drekkr	drank
drengr	fellow
drengskap	honour
drjúgum	greatly
dróttning	the-queen
drukkit	drunk
drukku	drinking
drykki	drank, drink
drykkju	drinking, drinks
dveljast	stay
dýrshorn	stag-horn

E, e

Old Norse	English
eða	but, or
ef	if
efna	carry-out
eftir	after, behind, remained, remaining
eiga	own
eigi	none, not, one
eignast	own
einhverja	one-such
einkum	especially
einn	one
einnhvern	one-such
eins	alone
einsætt	clearly
einskis	nothing
eitt	one
ek	I, I-am
ekki	not
eldist	old-is
elli	old-age
elligar	otherwise

Word List (Old Norse to English)

Old Norse	English
eltast	chased
em	am
en	and, as, But, than, that, then, while, who
enda	and, conclude, end
enga	no
engan	no, only
engi	none
engis	nothing
Englandsfari	England-Traveller (name)
engu	none
enn	but, still, then, was
enskis	no
er	am, as, had, have, is, it-is, that, was, were, what, when, where, which, who
erendlaust	errand-without
ert	are
ertu	are-you
eru	are, there-are, they, they-were, were

F, f

Old Norse	English
fá	gave, get, give, pay
faðir	father
fæ	give
fæð	sadness
fær	brought
færa	brought
færi	bring, travel, went
færið	bring
færir	brought
færr	accomplished, travel
fært	bringing
fagnaðartíðendi	good-news
fái	give
fáir	few
falar	bargain
falslaust	without-fraud
fám	a-few
fámæltr	of-few-words
fann	found
fara	go, going, travel, travelling, went
fararefnin	travel-goods
fari	travel
farir	travel
farit	travel, travelled
fars	travel
fastara	more-fixedly
fátt	few
fé	payment
fegnir	celebrated
fengi	found
fengit	got
fénu	wealth
ferðir	travel
ferr	goes, went
festa	fasten
fét	wealth
finnimst	found
fjárheimta	money-insisting
fjölði	many
fleiri	more
floti	floating
flytja	carried
fór	did, travelled, went
för	going
fórtu	went-you
förunauta	companions
förunautar	companions
föruneyti	companionship
fótum	feed
frá	from
frændum	father
fram	forward, forwards, from
framarla	forward
framgjarn	ambitious
fríðr	handsome
fullreynt	fully-tested
fund	find, meet, to-meet
fundust	met
fylgði	follow
fylgðina	following
fylgir	following
fylgja	follow
fyndist	found

Word List (Old Norse to English)

Old Norse	English
fyrir	along, before, for
fyrr	before
fyrra	the-first
fyrsta	first
fyrstu	first
fýsir	desire

G, g

Old Norse	English
gæði	good-things
gærkveld	last-night
gæta	take-care
gaf	gave
gáfu	gave
gáfuð	gave
gálga	gallows
galzt	payment
gamall	old
gamalmenni	old-men
ganga	go
Garðaríki	Gardariki (place)
gefa	give, to-give
gefinn	given
gegnum	through
gekk	went
gelzt	paid
gengr	going, went
gengu	went
gera	did, do, get, to-do
gerði	did
gerir	went
gerist	be
gerla	completely
gersimar	treasure, treasures
gersimum	treasure
gert	done
get	get
gjalda	pay
gjaldit	payment, the-payment
gjöfin	gift
gjöfina	the-gift
glaðari	gladness
glymr	echo
góð	good
goða	the-priest
góðr	good
greiða	assist
gulls	gold
gyldist	repay

H, h

Old Norse	English
hægt	possible
hæra	higher, highest
hæsta	highest
hættir	way
haf	sea
hafa	had, have, having, to-have, to-sea
hafði	had
hafi	had, has
hafið	have
hafir	have
hafs	sea
haft	had
halda	held, to-hold
haldast	hold
hálf	half
Halldór	Halldor (name)
Halldóri	Halldor (name)
Halldórr	Halldor (name)
Halldórs	Halldor (name), Halldor's (name)
hálm	straw, the-straw
halt	hold
haltu	hold-you
hann	he, him, it
hans	him, his
Harald	Harald (name)
Haraldi	Harald (name)
Haraldr	Harald (name)
Haralds	Harald (name)
Haraldsslátta	Harald's-money (name)
háseta	crew, sailors
hásetar	sailors
hásetum	sailors
háski	dangers
hausti	the-autumn

Word List (Old Norse to English)

Old Norse	English
heðan	from-here, hence
hefði	had
hefi	have
hefir	had, has, has-been, have, we-have
heilstan	thanks
heimfúsari	home-longing
heimta	drew
heimtir	got
heldr	hold, rather
helmings	half
helzt	rather
helzti	rather
hendi	hand
her	here
hér	forces, here
herra	lord
hét	named, promised, was-named
heyra	hear
heyrðuð	heard
heyrum	hear
hirðar	court
hirðina	guardsmen
hirðinni	court
hirðmaðr	court-man
hirðsiðum	king's-men-customs
hitt	find
hitta	find
hitti	found
hittir	found
Hjarðarholti	Hjardarholt (place)
hlaupa	to-run
hleypr	run
hljóp	ran
hlut	part, share
hluti	part, things
hlutr	part
hlutum	things
hlýða	listen-to
hlýs	warmth
höfðu	had
hófi	modest
hon	she
höndum	hand
honum	as-him, he, him, to-him
horn	horn
hornblástr	horn-blast
hornit	the-drinking-horn
hornsins	the-horn
hríð	awhile
hring	a-ring
hringingar	bell-ringing
hringingum	bell-ringing
hringinn	the-ring
hringja	ring
húðfat	hammock
hug	think
hurfu	disappeared
hús	house
hvárki	neither
hvárr	each
hvárt	each, how, which
hvat	what
hvégi	which
hver	where
hverju	each
hverjum	who
hvern	which
hverr	each, who
hvers	how, what
hversu	how-so
hvert	each
hví	why
hygg	think

I, i

Old Norse	English
illa	badly, ill
in	the
inn	inside, the

Í, í

Old Norse	English
í	about, at, from, in, into, of, out-of, that, to, will, with
ígangsklæði	travelling-clothes

Word List (Old Norse to English)

Old Norse	English
Ísland	Iceland (place)
Íslandi	Icelander (name)
Íslands	Iceland (place)
íslenzkan	Icelander

J, j

Old Norse	English
jafnfylginn	equally-following
jafnmjök	equally-much
jafntraustan	equally-trustworthy
jafntraustir	equally-trustworthy
jóla	Yule (name)
jólanna	Yule (name)
jólin	Yule (name)
Jólum	Yule (name)

K, k

Old Norse	English
kæma	come
kærleikum	dearly-loved
kaf	overboard
kalla	called
kallat	called
kann	can, know
kappgjarn	self-willed
kaupa	purchase
Kaupangi	Kaupang (place)
kaupferðir	trading-voyages
kaupir	bought
kaupmaðr	trading-man
kaupmenn	merchants, the-merchants, the-traders
kaupsveinar	trading-men
kaupverðsins	ship's-worth
kemr	came
kennduð	taught
kertisveinar	court-men
kjósa	choose
klokkurum	clocks
knörr	ship
kom	came
koma	came, come, coming
komið	come
kominn	come, coming
komir	come
kómu	came
konung	the-king
konunga	the-king
konungi	king, the-king, to-the-king
konungr	king, the-king
konungs	the-king, the-king's
konungsmenn	the-kings-men
konungsskipinu	the-king's-ship
kopars	copper
kostar	choice
kosti	benefit
krefja	demand
ksonungs	the-king's
kunnigt	known
kvað	said
kvaddi	called
kvaðst	said
kveld	evening
kyrrt	peace

L, l

Old Norse	English
lá	lay
lætr	behave, leave, let
lagi	had
land	land, the-land
landa	lands
landi	land, lands, the-land
lands	land
landtjald	land-tents
langskip	longships
lát	let-it
láta	allow, have, losing
láti	have
launuð	repaid
leggi	lay
leggja	grant
leggjum	lay
leggr	laid
leið	pass, passed, way
leita	seek
leitat	consider

Word List (Old Norse to English)

Old Norse	English
lendir	landed
lendr	land
lendra	is-paid, payment
lengi	long
lengr	longer
lét	had
léti	let
léttlætiskonum	prostitutes
leyfa	allow
leyfi	leave
lézt	had
liði	crew, men
liðit	passed
líðr	passed
lifa	life
líka	like
líkaði	liked
líta	look
lítill	little
litlu	little
lítr	looked
litt	little
lítt	little
lízt	appears
loftinu	the-air
lögðu	laid
logizt	cheated
lokit	ended
lönd	land
löng	long
lygi	lie
lyndi	temper
Lyrgju	Lyrgja (place)
lýstr	struck

M, m

Old Norse	English
má	may
maðr	a-man, man
mæðumst	tired
mælt	spoken, spoken-of
mælti	spoke, spoke-to
mæltuð	spoke
mætti	may, might, might
mál	conversed, matter, measure
mála	matter, payment, payment
málagjöfna	payment
málann	payment
málanum	payment
málasilfrit	silverware
máli	matter, payment, speak
mann	man
manna	men, people, people's
mannháska	human-danger
marga	many
margr	many
matar	food
máttu	may, may-you
með	along, between, with
mega	may
meir	more
meira	more
meiri	greater, more
melrakkabelgi	arctic-fox-furs
menn	men, people
mér	me, to-me, with-me
mesta	most
mesti	most
mik	me
mikill	a-great, great
mikinn	greatly, much
mikit	huge
mikla	much
Miklagarði	The-Great-City (place)
miklu	a-great, much
miklum	much
milli	between
mín	me, mine
mína	mine
minn	mine
minna	less
minni	mine
mínu	my
mislíkaði	misliked
mitt	mine, my
mjök	much

Word List (Old Norse to English)

Old Norse	English
mönnum	people
morgun	morning, the-morning
mörk	a-mark
mót	return
móti	meet, meeting
mótinu	the-meeting
móts	meet
mótsins	the-meeting
möttulsskauti	cloak-lap
mun	could, shall, should, would
muni	shall
munkat	shall
munt	must
muntu	should
munum	shall, should
myndi	should, would
myndir	would
myndu	would
myrgininn	morning

N, n

Old Norse	English
næst	next
næsta	next, next-to
næstum	before
nætr	night
náliga	nearly
nauðgat	force
nauðsyn	necessity
né	nor
neðan	below
neitt	nothing
nema	except, take
neyta	use
neytti	consumed
Nið	Nid (place)
níðist	down
niðr	below, down
nóga	enough
nökkur	something
nökkura	some
nökkurum	some
nökkut	something, somewhat
norðr	north

Old Norse	English
Nóreg	Norway (place)
Noregi	Norway (place)
Nóregi	Norway (place)
Nóregs	Norway (place)
norrænir	Norwegians
nótt	night
nú	now

O, o

Old Norse	English
of	over
oft	often
oftar	frequent, more-often
ok	also, and
okkar	ours
okkr	our, us
orð	word, words, word-to
orðaframkast	outburst
orði	word
orðsending	word-sending
oss	to-us, us

Ó, ó

Old Norse	English
ófriðar	hostilities
ófriðinn	un-peace
ófriðr	un-peace
ófúss	unwilling
óglaðari	un-gladness
ógladdist	un-glad
ómakliga	undeservedly
ómjúkr	un-bending
ónýttir	un-used
ór	from, out-of
órráða	solution
Ósló	Oslo (place)
ósýnt	unseen
ótiginn	un-high-born
óvingjarnliga	unfriendly

Ö, ö

Old Norse	English
öðru	a-second

Word List (Old Norse to English)

Old Norse	English
öðrum	other
öllu	all
öllum	all

P, p

Old Norse	English
prettum	trick

R, r

Old Norse	English
ráð	advise, the-matter
ráða	prevail
ráðagerðir	advice-giving
ráðast	appoint, arrange
ráðist	decide
ráðit	hired
ræðr	leading
ræðst	commanded
reiði	anger
reiðist	commanded
rekit	thrown
rekkju	bed
reyki	smoke
reyna	know
ríki	kingdom
ró	rest
rúmi	seat
rúms	room

S, s

Old Norse	English
sá	saw, so
sæmð	honour
sæmiligt	the-same
sættast	reconcile
sagði	said
sagt	is-said, said
sakar	the-sake-of
saman	together
samir	so
sat	sat, stayed
satt	be-true, true
sátu	sat, sat
sé	is, see, so
seg	say
segir	said, told
segja	say, told
segl	the-sails
seilast	to-reach
sein	late
seint	late, slow, slowly
sel	flip
sem	as, that, was, which
semja	negotiate
senda	send
sendi	sent
sér	be, for, he, him, himself, saw, see, themselves
sessunautar	sitting-together
setið	set
setja	sit
settust	sat
sex	six
síð	later
síðan	afterwards, since, then
síðar	afterwards, later
síðast	the-last
síðkveldum	late-evening
síðr	less
sigldu	sailed
siglingum	sailing
Sigurðr	Sigurd (name)
sik	him
silfr	silver
silfrinu	the-silver
silfrit	the-silver
sín	him, theirs
sína	his
sínar	theirs
sinn	he, his
sinni	his, themselves, time, yourself
síns	his
sínu	his, their
sínum	his
sitja	settle
sitr	sat

Word List (Old Norse to English)

Old Norse	English
sitt	his
sízt	least
sja	see
sjá	see, so
sjálfir	themselves
sjám	we-see
skaða	damages
skal	shall
skálum	bowl
skammt	short-distance
skap	mood
skapi	mood
skapkers	large-vessel
skaplyndi	mood-temper
skark	noise
skerit	a-rock
skilðust	separated
skilja	separate
skilnaðr	parting
skilr	separated
skip	a-ship, ship, ships, the-ship
skipagangr	shipping
skipan	ships
skipi	a-ship, ship
skipinu	ship, the-ship
skipit	ship, the-ship
skips	a-ship, ships
skipsins	ship
skipstjórn	ship-steering
skipstjórnar	ship-steer
skipum	ships
skipun	crew
skipverja	the-crew
skíran	cleared
skírt	pure
skjótt	swift, swiftly
skorti	shortly
skotit	launched
skulu	should
skuluð	should
skulum	shall
skyggt	shaded
skyldi	should
skyldu	should
skyli	shall
skyti	shot
skýtr	launched
sleit	broken-up
sleitiliga	unfairly
slíkra	such
slíkri	such
slíkt	such
slíku	such
slótt	struck
snemma	early, soon
Snorra	Snorri (name)
Snorrason	Snorrason (name)
Snorrasyni	Snorrason (name)
snúa	turned
sofa	sleep
sögð	told
sögðu	said
sóma	honour
sömu	the-same
spilli	spoil
spurði	asked
spyrr	asked
stað	replace
stafninn	the-prow
stefnið	heading
stendr	stands, stood
stirðlæti	hard-temper
stjórnar	steer
stóð	stood
stóðu	stood
stofunni	chamber
stórættaðr	of-high-family
stórmennsku	greatness
strangt	strange
stríðu	stressful
stuttorðr	short-worded
stygglyndr	quick-tempered
stýrði	steered
stýrimaðr	steersman
stýrimanns	the-steersman
styrkastr	strongest
stytti	short
suðr	south
sumarit	summer
sumir	some

Word List (Old Norse to English)

Old Norse	English
sumrum	summers
sundr	separate
svá	so
svaf	slept
sváfu	slept
svarar	answered
sveinar	fellows
Sveini	Svein (name)
sveinn	fellow, Svein (name), the-fellow
svívirðing	disgrace
svivirðliga	dishonourable
svívirðr	dishonourable
sýndist	seemed
synir	sons
sýnist	seemed
sýnum	in-appearance
sýr	Sow

T, t

Old Norse	English
taka	take
tala	speak
tek	take
tekit	taken
tekr	took
tíðast	swiftly
tíðendi	tidings
til	about, for, to, until
títt	immediately
tízka	custom
tók	took
tóku	took
tólf	twelve
trúa	believe

Þ, þ

Old Norse	English
þá	them, then
þætti	seems
þakkaði	thanked
þakkar	thanked
þangat	from-there
þann	it, then
þannug	that-way
þar	there, there, they
þarf	needed
þat	it, that, this
þatki	that-not
þau	them, then, then
þegar	straightaway, straightaway, there
þeim	of-them, them, they
þeir	the, there, they
þekkjast	accept
þenna	that
þér	to-you, you, you-to
þess	is-this, like-this, that, these, this, those
þessi	these, this
þessu	this
þessum	those
þetta	it, that, this
þik	you
þín	your
þína	yours
þínar	you
þinn	your, yours
þínum	yours
þitt	yours
þjóna	serve
þjónat	served
þjónusta	service
þjónustu	service
þjónustumenn	servants
þó	though
þokkar	favours
þörf	needed
Þóri	Thorir (name)
Þórir	Thorir (name), Thorir (name)
Þóris	Thorir's (name)
þótt	though
þóttist	thought
Þrándheimi	Trondheim (place)
Þrándheims	Trondheim (place)
þrenna	treble
þrjú	three
þú	you
þurfa	needed, you-need

Word List (Old Norse to English)

Old Norse	English
því	accordingly, because, of, that, therefore, with
þykki	think, thought
þykkir	seemed, thinks
þykkist	think
þykkja	think
þykkjast	consider
þykkjumst	think

U, u

Old Norse	English
um	about
umræða	discussion
undan	away-from, from-under, under
undir	under
undirhlutrinn	the-under-part
unnit	deserved
upp	up, upped
uppi	up
upplenzkr	an-Upplander
upplost	false-rumour
urðu	became

Ú, ú

Old Norse	English
út	out, out-of
útan	out
útferð	out-travelling
úti	outside

V, v

Old Norse	English
vægð	grace
vændiskonum	prostitutes
vænna	expected
væri	had, was
vakna	awoke
vaknar	awoke
vald	power
vanði	custom
vandskipaðr	difficult
vant	difficult, expected
vápndjarfastr	weapons-bold
vápnum	weapons
var	was, were
vár	our
vára	going, spring
varð	became, was
varðveita	guard-over
várit	spring
varla	hardly
várt	ours
váru	were
vátir	wet
váveifliga	unexpected
vega	weigh
vegr	way
veit	know
veita	grant, lead
veizlum	the-feasts
veizlur	feasts
veizt	know
veiztu	know-you
vel	well
ver	be
vér	we
vera	be, becoming, being, is, it-be
verð	worth
verða	be, to-be
verðr	came, worth
verðum	worth
verit	be, been, being, had-been
verja	spend
verr	worse
verri	worse
verst	becomes
vert	worth, worthy
vetr	winter
vetrinn	winter
vexti	well-built
við	against, with
víghug	killing-mind
Vík	Vik (place)
vil	will, wish
vildi	willed, wish, wished

Word List (Old Norse to English)

Old Norse	English
vilgis	very
vili	willed
vilja	wish
viljum	wish, wish-to
vill	willed, wish, wished, wished-to, wishes
vinar	friend
vináttu	friendship
vinda	wind
vingan	friendship
vingjarnlig	friendly
vinna	to-win-over
vinr	friend
vinveitt	favourable
virðing	honour, worthiness
víst	certainly
vistum	provisions
vísu	certainly
vit	with
vita	certainly, know
víti	punishment, signalled
vitið	know
vítin	penalty
vítishornit	penalty-horn
vítit	penalty, the-penalty
vitni	testimony
víttr	penalty, reprimanded
vizkr	wise

Y, y

Old Norse	English
yðr	you
yðrar	yours
yðvars	yours
yfir	over
yfirbragði	complexion
ykkarr	with-you
ykkr	you-two
ykkra	yours
yrði	became

Ý, ý

Old Norse	English
ýkva	veer
ýmissa	various

Word List *(English to Old Norse)*

English	Old Norse

A, a

English	Old Norse
a-ban	*bann*
about	*á, í, til, um*
accept	*þekkjast*
access	*atgang*
accomplished	*færr*
accordingly	*því*
advice-giving	*ráðagerðir*
advise	*ráð*
a-few	*fám*
after	*aftr, eftir*
afterwards	*síðan, síðar*
against	*við*
age	*ævi*
a-great	*mikill, miklu*
all	*allir, allir, allra, allt, allt, öllu, öllum*
all-long	*alllangt*
allow	*láta, leyfa*
all-prepared	*albúnir*
alone	*eins*
along	*fyrir, með*
also	*ok*
am	*em, er*
a-man	*maðr*
a-mark	*mörk*
ambitious	*framgjarn*
ancestry	*ætt*
and	*á, en, enda, ok, 0*
anger	*reiði*
another	*annan, annan, annars*
answered	*svarar*
an-Upplander	*upplenzkr*
appears	*lízt*
appoint	*ráðast*
arctic-fox-furs	*melrakkabelgi*
are	*ert, eru*
are-you	*ertu*
a-ring	*hring*
a-rock	*skerit*
arrange	*ráðast*
as	*á, en, er, sem*
a-second	*öðru*
as-him	*honum*
a-ship	*skip, skipi, skips*
asked	*beiða, beitt, biðr, spurði, spyrr*
asks	*beiðir*
assist	*greiða*
at	*á, at, í*
a-trick	*brögð*
away	*brott*
away-from	*undan*
away-prepared	*brautbúnaði*
awhile	*hríð*
awoke	*vakna, vaknar*

B, b

English	Old Norse
back	*aftr*
badly	*illa*
ban	*bannar*
Bard (name)	*Bárðr*
bargain	*falar*
be	*gerist, sér, ver, vera, verða, verit*
bear	*bera, beri*
bears	*berr*
became	*urðu, varð, yrði*
because	*því*
becomes	*verst*
becoming	*vera*
bed	*rekkju*
been	*verit*
before	*áðr, fyrir, fyrr, næstum*
began	*byrjaði*
behave	*lætr*
behind	*eftir*
being	*vera, verit*
believe	*trúa*
bell-ringing	*hringingar, hringingum*
below	*neðan, niðr*

Word List (English to Old Norse)

English	*Old Norse*
benefit	*kosti*
best	*bergst, bezt, bezta*
be-true	*satt*
better	*betr, betra*
between	*með, milli*
bid	*báðu, biðr*
bold	*djörfung*
bore	*bar*
both	*báðum, bæði*
bought	*kaupir*
bowl	*skálum*
Bratteyar (place)	*Bröttueyri*
breaking	*brjótist*
bring	*færi, færið*
bringing	*bar, fært*
broken-up	*sleit*
brought	*fær, færa, færir*
burnt	*brennda*
but	*eða, en, enn*

C, c

English	*Old Norse*
called	*kalla, kallat, kvaddi*
calling	*ákalsi*
came	*kemr, kom, koma, kómu, verðr*
can	*kann*
carried	*berr, flytja*
carry-out	*efna*
celebrated	*fegnir*
certainly	*víst, vísu, vita*
chamber	*stofunni*
changed	*breytt*
chased	*eltast*
cheated	*logizt*
choice	*kostar*
choose	*kjósa*
cleared	*skíran*
clearly	*einsætt*
cloak-lap	*möttulsskauti*
clocks	*klokkurum*
come	*kæma, koma, komið, kominn, komir*
coming	*koma, kominn*
commanded	*ræðst, reiðist*
companions	*förunauta, förunautar*
companionship	*föruneyti*
completely	*gerla*
complexion	*yfirbragði*
conclude	*enda*
consider	*leitat, þykkjast*
consumed	*neytti*
conversed	*mál*
copper	*kopars*
could	*mun*
court	*hirðar, hirðinni*
court-man	*hirðmaðr*
court-men	*kertisveinar*
crew	*áhöfnina, háseta, liði, skipun*
custom	*tízka, vanði*

D, d

English	*Old Norse*
damages	*skaða*
dangers	*háski*
Danish-forces	*danaher*
day	*dag, dagr*
days	*dögum*
dearly-loved	*kærleikum*
decide	*ráðist*
deeming	*dóm*
demand	*krefja*
Denmark (place)	*Danmerkr*
deserved	*unnit*
desire	*fýsir*
did	*fór, gera, gerði*
difficult	*vandskipaðr, vant*
direction	*beint*
disappeared	*hurfu*
discussion	*umræða*
disgrace	*svívirðing*
dishonourable	*sviviðliga, svívirðr*
do	*gera*
done	*gert*
down	*níðist, niðr*
drank	*drakk, drekka, drekkr, drykki*
drew	*heimta*
drink	*drekk, drekka, drykki*

Word List (English to Old Norse)

English	Old Norse
drinking	*drukku, drykkju*
drinks	*drykkju*
drunk	*drukkit*

E, e

English	Old Norse
each	*hvárr, hvárt, hverju, hverr, hvert*
early	*snemma*
early-riser	*árrisull*
east	*austan, austr*
echo	*glymr*
eighth	*átti*
end	*enda*
ended	*lokit*
England-Traveller (name)	*Englandsfari*
enough	*nóga*
equally-following	*jafnfylginn*
equally-much	*jafnmjök*
equally-trustworthy	*jafntraustan, jafntraustir*
errand-without	*erendlaust*
especially	*einkum*
evening	*aftan, aftna, kveld*
except	*nema*
expected	*vænna, vant*

F, f

English	Old Norse
fair-wind	*byrr*
false-rumour	*upplost*
farmed	*bjó*
fasten	*festa*
father	*faðir, frændum*
favourable	*vinveitt*
favours	*þokkar*
feasts	*veizlur*
feed	*fótum*
fellow	*drengr, sveinn*
fellows	*sveinar*
few	*fáir, fátt*
find	*fund, hitt, hitta*
first	*fyrsta, fyrstu*

English	Old Norse
flip	*sel*
floating	*floti*
follow	*fylgði, fylgja*
following	*fylgðina, fylgir*
food	*matar*
for	*fyrir, sér, til*
force	*nauðgat*
forces	*hér*
foreclose	*bregða*
forward	*fram, framarla*
forwards	*fram*
found	*fann, fengi, finnimst, fyndist, hitti, hittir*
frequent	*oftar*
friend	*vinar, vinr*
friendly	*vingjarnlig*
friendship	*vináttu, vingan*
from	*af, af, frá, fram, í, ór*
from-here	*heðan*
from-there	*þangat*
from-under	*undan*
fully-tested	*fullreynt*
furs	*belgi*

G, g

English	Old Norse
gallows	*gálga*
Gardariki (place)	*Garðaríki*
gave	*bar, fá, gaf, gáfu, gáfuð*
get	*fá, gera, get*
gift	*gjöfin*
give	*fá, fæ, fái, gefa*
given	*gefinn*
gladness	*glaðari*
go	*fara, ganga*
goes	*ferr*
going	*fara, för, gengr, vára*
gold	*gulls*
good	*góð, góðr*
good-news	*fagnaðartíðendi*
good-things	*gæði*
got	*fengit, heimtir*
grace	*vægð*
grant	*leggja, veita*

Word List (English to Old Norse)

English	*Old Norse*	English	*Old Norse*
great	*mikill*	himself	*sér*
greater	*meiri*	hired	*ráðit*
greatly	*drjúgum, mikinn*	his	*hans, sína, sinn, sinni, síns, sínu, sínum, sitt*
greatness	*stórmennsku*		
guard-over	*varðveita*		
guardsmen	*hirðina*	Hjardarholt (place)	*Hjarðarholti*
		hold	*haldast, halt, heldr*

H, h

		hold-you	*haltu*
		home-longing	*heimfúsari*
had	*á, átti, er, hafa, hafði, hafi, haft, hefði, hefir, höfðu, lagi, lét, lézt, væri*	honour	*drengskap, sæmð, sóma, virðing*
		horn	*horn*
		horn-blast	*hornblástr*
		hostilities	*ófriðar*
had-been	*verit*	house	*hús*
half	*hálf, helmings*	how	*hvárt, hvers*
Halldor (name)	*Halldór, Halldóri, Halldórr, Halldórs*	how-so	*hversu*
		huge	*mikit*
Halldor's (name)	*Halldórs*	human-danger	*mannháska*
hammock	*húðfat*		
hand	*hendi, höndum*		

I, i

handsome	*fríðr*		
happiest	*blíðast*		
happily	*blíðligr*	I	*ek*
Harald (name)	*Harald, Haraldi, Haraldr, Haralds*	I-am	*ek*
		Iceland (place)	*Ísland, Íslands*
Harald's-money (name)	*Haraldsslátta*	Icelander	*íslenzkan*
		Icelander (name)	*Íslandi*
hardly	*varla*	if	*ef*
hard-temper	*stirðlæti*	ill	*illa*
has	*hafi, hefir*	immediately	*títt*
has-been	*hefir*	in	*á, at, í*
have	*er, hafa, hafið, hafir, hefi, hefir, láta, láti*	in-appearance	*sýnum*
		in-on	*at*
having	*hafa*	inside	*inn*
he	*hann, honum, sér, sinn*	intend	*ætla*
		intended	*ætlaði, ætlar, ætlast, ætlat*
heading	*stefnið*		
hear	*heyra, heyrum*	intends	*ætlar*
heard	*heyrðuð*	into	*í*
held	*halda*	invitation	*boð*
hence	*heðan*	is	*á, er, sé, vera*
here	*her, hér*	is-paid	*lendra*
higher	*hæra*	is-said	*sagt*
highest	*hæra, hæsta*	is-this	*þess*
him	*hann, hans, honum, sér, sik, sín*		

42

Word List (English to Old Norse)

English	*Old Norse*	English	*Old Norse*
it	*at, hann, þann, þat, þetta*	let-it	*lát*
it-be	*vera*	lie	*lygi*
it-is	*er*	life	*lifa*
		like	*líka*
		liked	*líkaði*
		like-this	*þess*
		listen-to	*hlýða*

J, j

joyful	*blíðu*

little	*lítill, litlu, litt, lítt*
long	*lengi, löng*
longer	*lengr*
longships	*langskip*
look	*líta*
looked	*lítr*
lord	*herra*
losing	*láta*
Lyrgja (place)	*Lyrgju*

K, k

English	*Old Norse*
Kaupang (place)	*Kaupangi*
keep-asking	*brekar*
killing-mind	*víghug*
king	*konungi, konungr*
kingdom	*ríki*
king-of-Denmark	*danakonungr*
king's-men-customs	*hirðsiðum*
know	*kann, reyna, veit, veizt, vita, vitið*
known	*kunnigt*
know-you	*veiztu*

M, m

English	*Old Norse*
man	*maðr, mann*
many	*fjölði, marga, margr*
matter	*mál, mála, máli*
may	*má, mætti, máttu, mega*
may-you	*máttu*
me	*mér, mik, mín*
measure	*mál*
meet	*fund, móti, móts*
meeting	*móti*
men	*liði, manna, menn*
merchants	*kaupmenn*
merchant-ship	*byrðing*
met	*fundust*
might	*mætti, mætti*
mine	*mín, mína, minn, minni, mitt*
misliked	*mislíkaði*
modest	*hófi*
moment	*bili*
money-insisting	*fjárheimta*
mood	*skap, skapi*
mood-temper	*skaplyndi*
more	*fleiri, meir, meira, meiri*
more-fixedly	*fastara*

L, l

English	*Old Norse*
laid	*leggr, lögðu*
land	*land, landi, lands, lendr, lönd*
landed	*lendir*
lands	*landa, landi*
land-tents	*landtjald*
large-vessel	*skapkers*
last-night	*gærkveld*
late	*sein, seint*
late-evening	*síðkveldum*
later	*síð, síðar*
launched	*skotit, skýtr*
lay	*lá, leggi, leggjum*
lead	*veita*
leading	*ræðr*
least	*sízt*
leave	*lætr, leyfi*
less	*minna, síðr*
let	*lætr, léti*

Word List (English to Old Norse)

English	*Old Norse*	English	*Old Norse*
more-often	*oftar*	on	*á*
morning	*morgun, myrgininn*	one	*eigi, einn, eitt*
most	*mesta, mesti*	one-such	*einhverja, einnhvern*
much	*mikinn, mikla, miklu, miklum, mjök*	only	*engan*
		on-the	*á*
must	*munt*	or	*eða*
my	*mínu, mitt*	Oslo (place)	*Ósló*
		other	*áðr, aðra, aðrir, annarra, annarri, öðrum*

N, n

		otherwise	*elligar*
named	*hét*	ounces	*aura*
nearly	*náliga*	our	*okkr, vár*
necessity	*nauðsyn*	ours	*okkar, várt*
needed	*þarf, þörf, þurfa*	out	*út, útan*
negotiate	*semja*	outburst	*orðaframkast*
neither	*hvárki*	out-of	*í, ór, út*
next	*næst, næsta*	outside	*úti*
next-to	*næsta*	outspoken	*bermæltr*
Nid (place)	*Nið*	out-travelling	*útferð*
night	*nætr, nótt*	over	*of, yfir*
no	*enga, engan, enskis*	overboard	*kaf*
noise	*skark*	own	*eiga, eignast*
none	*eigi, engi, engu*		
nor	*né*		
north	*norðr*		

P, p

Norway (place)	*Nóreg, Noregi, Nóregi, Nóregs*		
		paid	*gelzt*
Norwegians	*norrænir*	part	*hlut, hluti, hlutr*
not	*eigi, ekki*	parting	*skilnaðr*
nothing	*einskis, engis, neitt*	pass	*leið*
now	*nú*	passed	*leið, liðit, líðr*
		pay	*fá, gjalda*
		payment	*fé, galzt, gjaldit, lendra, mála, mála, málagjöfna, málann, málanum, máli*

O, o

		peace	*kyrrt*
of	*á, af, af, at, í, því*	penalty	*vítin, vítit, víttr*
of-all	*allra*	penalty-horn	*vítishornit*
of-few-words	*fámæltr*	people	*manna, menn, mönnum*
of-high-family	*stórættaðr*		
often	*oft*	people's	*manna*
of-them	*þeim*	possible	*hægt*
old	*gamall*	power	*vald*
old-age	*elli*	preparations	*bjuggu, búnaðinn*
old-is	*eldist*		
old-men	*gamalmenni*		

Word List (English to Old Norse)

English	Old Norse
prepared	*búa, búinn, búit, býr, býstu*
prepares	*býst*
prevail	*ráða*
promised	*hét*
promising-wind	*byrvænligt*
prostitutes	*léttlætiskonum, vændiskonum*
provisions	*vistum*
punishment	*víti*
purchase	*kaupa*
pure	*skírt*

Q, q

English	Old Norse
quick-tempered	*stygglyndr*

R, r

English	Old Norse
ran	*hljóp*
rather	*heldr, helzt, helzti*
reacted	*brygði*
readied	*bjóst*
reconcile	*sættast*
remained	*eftir*
remaining	*eftir*
repaid	*launuð*
repaired	*bætt*
repay	*gyldist*
replace	*stað*
reprimanded	*víttr*
resolved	*alhugat*
rest	*ró*
return	*mót*
ring	*hringja*
room	*rúms*
run	*hleypr*

S, s

English	Old Norse
sadness	*fæð*
said	*kvað, kvaðst, sagði, sagt, segir, sögðu*
sailed	*sigldu*
sailing	*siglingum*
sailors	*háseta, hásetar, hásetum*
sat	*sat, sátu, sátu, settust, sitr*
saw	*sá, sér*
say	*seg, segja*
sea	*haf, hafs*
seat	*rúmi*
see	*sé, sér, sja, sjá*
seek	*leita*
seemed	*sýndist, sýnist, þykkir*
seems	*þætti*
self-willed	*kappgjarn*
send	*senda*
sent	*sendi*
separate	*skilja, sundr*
separated	*skilðust, skilr*
servants	*þjónustumenn*
serve	*þjóna*
served	*þjónat*
service	*þjónusta, þjónustu*
set	*setið*
settle	*bú, byggja, sitja*
settled	*bjó*
shaded	*skyggt*
shall	*mun, muni, munkat, munum, skal, skulum, skyli*
share	*hlut*
she	*hon*
ship	*knörr, skip, skipi, skipinu, skipit, skipsins*
shipping	*skipagangr*
ships	*skip, skipan, skips, skipum*
ship-steer	*skipstjórnar*
ship-steering	*skipstjórn*
ship's-worth	*kaupverðsins*
short	*stytti*
short-distance	*skammt*
shortly	*skorti*
short-worded	*stuttorðr*
shot	*skyti*

Word List (English to Old Norse)

English	*Old Norse*	English	*Old Norse*
should	mun, muntu, munum, myndi, skulu, skuluð, skyldi, skyldu	straightaway	þegar
		straight-away	þegar
		strange	strangt
signalled	víti	straw	hálm
Sigurd (name)	Sigurðr	stress	álaga
silver	silfr	stressful	stríðu
silverware	málasilfrit	strongest	styrkastr
since	síðan	struck	lýstr, slótt
sit	setja	such	slíkra, slíkri, slíkt, slíku
sitting-together	sessunautar		
six	sex	summer	sumarit
sleep	sofa	summers	sumrum
slept	svaf, sváfu	suppose	ætla
slow	seint	Svein (name)	Sveini, Sveinn
slowly	seint	swift	skjótt
smoke	reyki	swiftly	skjótt, tíðast
Snorrason (name)	Snorrason, Snorrasyni		

T, t

English	*Old Norse*
Snorri (name)	Snorra
so	sá, samir, sé, sjá, svá
solution	órráða
some	nökkura, nökkurum, sumir
something	nökkur, nökkut
somewhat	nökkut
sons	synir
soon	snemma
south	suðr
Sow	sýr
speak	máli, tala
spend	verja
spoil	spilli
spoke	mælti, mæltuð
spoken	mælt
spoken-of	mælt
spoke-to	mælti
spring	vára, várit
stag-horn	dýrshorn
stands	stendr
stay	dveljast
stayed	sat
steer	stjórnar
steered	stýrði
steersman	stýrimaðr
still	enn
stood	stendr, stóð, stóðu

English	*Old Norse*
take	nema, taka, tek
take-care	gæta
taken	tekit
taught	kennduð
temper	lyndi
testimony	vitni
than	en
thanked	þakkaði, þakkar
thanks	heilstan
that	á, at, en, er, í, sem, þat, þenna, þess, þetta, því
that-not	þatki
that-way	þannug
the	á, at, in, inn, þeir
the-air	loftinu
the-anchor	ákkeri
the-autumn	hausti
the-city	bænum
the-cockerel	árgalinn
the-crew	skipverja
the-day	daginn
the-drinking-horn	hornit
the-feasts	veizlum
the-fellow	sveinn
the-first	fyrra

46

Word List (English to Old Norse)

English	Old Norse	English	Old Norse
the-gift	gjöfina	they-were	eru
The-Great-City (place)	Miklagarði	things	hluti, hlutum
the-horn	hornsins	think	hug, hygg, þykki, þykkist, þykkja, þykkjumst
their	sínu		
theirs	sín, sínar	thinks	þykkir
the-king	konung, konunga, konungi, konungr, konungs	this	á, at, þat, þess, þessi, þessu, þetta
		this-town	bænum
the-king's	konungs, ksonungs	Thorir (name)	Þóri, Þórir, Þórir
the-kings-men	konungsmenn	Thorir's (name)	Þóris
the-king's-ship	konungsskipinu	those	þess, þessum
the-land	land, landi	though	þó, þótt
the-last	síðast	thought	þóttist, þykki
them	þá, þau, þeim	three	þrjú
the-matter	ráð	through	gegnum
the-meeting	mótinu, mótsins	thrown	rekit
the-merchants	kaupmenn	tidings	tíðendi
the-morning	morgun	tied-up	bindr
themselves	sér, sinni, sjálfir	time	sinni
then	á, en, enn, síðan, þá, þann, þau, þau	tired	mæðumst
		to	á, at, í, til
the-next	annan	to-be	verða
the-payment	gjaldit	to-come	at
the-penalty	vítit	to-do	gera
the-priest	goða	to-drink	drekka
the-prow	stafninn	together	saman
the-queen	dróttning	to-give	gefa
there	þar, þar, þegar, þeir	to-have	hafa
there-are	eru	to-him	honum
therefore	því	to-hold	halda
the-ring	hringinn	told	segir, segja, sögð
the-river	ánni	to-me	mér
the-sails	segl	to-meet	fund
the-sake-of	sakar	took	tekr, tók, tóku
the-same	sæmiligt, sömu	to-reach	seilast
these	þess, þessi	to-run	hlaupa
the-ship	skip, skipinu, skipit	to-sea	hafa
the-silver	silfrinu, silfrit	to-the-king	konungi
the-steersman	stýrimanns	to-us	oss
the-straw	hálm	to-win-over	vinna
the-tow-boat	báti	town	bæinn
the-town	bænum	townspeople	bæjarmenn
the-traders	kaupmenn	to-you	þér
the-under-part	undirhlutrinn	trading-man	kaupmaðr
they	eru, þar, þeim, þeir	trading-men	kaupsveinar

Word List (English to Old Norse)

English	*Old Norse*	English	*Old Norse*
trading-voyages	kaupferðir	very	vilgis
travel	færi, færr, fara, fari, farir, farit, fars, ferðir	Vik (place)	Vík
		violated	brotin
travel-goods	fararefnin		
travelled	farit, fór		
travelling	fara		
travelling-clothes	ígangsklæði		

W, w

English	*Old Norse*
treasure	gersimar, gersimum
treasures	gersimar
treble	þrenna
trick	prettum
Trondheim (place)	Þrándheimi, Þrándheims
true	
trumpet-blown	blásit
turbulence	aga
turned	snúa
twelve	tólf

English	*Old Norse*
wait	bíð, bíða, biðleika,
warmth	hlýs
warn	ávíta
was	enn, er, sem, væri, var, varð
was-named	hét
way	hættir, leið, vegr
we	vér
wealth	fénu, fét
weapons	vápnum
weapons-bold	vápndjarfastr
we-have	hefir
weigh	vega
well	vel
well-built	vexti
went	færi, fara, ferr, fór, gekk, gengr, gengu, gerir
went-you	fórtu
were	er, eru, var, váru
we-see	sjám
wet	vátir
what	er, hvat, hvers
when	er
where	er, hver
which	er, hvárt, hvégi, hvern, sem
while	en
who	en, er, hverjum, hverr
why	hví
will	í, vil
willed	vildi, vili, vill
wind	vinda
winter	vetr, vetrinn
wise	vizkr
wish	vil, vildi, vilja, viljum, vill
wished	vildi, vill
wished-to	vill

U, u

English	*Old Norse*
un-bending	ómjúkr
under	undan, undir
undeservedly	ómakliga
unexpected	váveifliga
unfairly	sleitiliga
unfriendly	óvingjarnliga
un-glad	ógladdist
un-gladness	óglaðari
un-high-born	ótiginn
un-peace	ófriðinn, ófriðr
unseen	ósýnt
until	til
un-used	ónýttir
unwilling	ófúss
up	upp, uppi
upped	upp
us	okkr, oss
use	neyta

V, v

English	*Old Norse*
various	ýmissa
veer	ýkva

Word List (English to Old Norse)

English	*Old Norse*
wishes	*vill*
wish-to	*viljum*
with	*í, með, því, við, vit*
with-me	*mér*
without-fraud	*falslaust*
with-you	*ykkarr*
word	*orð, orði*
words	*orð*
word-sending	*orðsending*
word-to	*orð*
worried-face	*áhyggjusvip*
worse	*verr, verri*
worth	*verð, verðr, verðum, vert*
worthiness	*virðing*
worthy	*vert*
would	*mun, myndi, myndir, myndu*

Y, y

you	*þér, þik, þínar, þú, yðr*
you-need	*þurfa*
your	*þín, þinn*
yours	*þína, þinn, þínum, þitt, yðrar, yðvars, ykkra*
yourself	*sinni*
you-to	*þér*
you-two	*ykkr*
Yule (name)	*jóla, jólanna, jólin, Jólum*

The Tale of Halldor Snorrason II (Old Icelandic)

The Tale of Halldor Snorrason II (*Old Icelandic*)

Old Icelandic	Literal	English
1	**1**	**1**
Halldór Snorrason hafði verið út í Miklagarði með Haraldi sem áður er sagt og kom í Noreg með honum austan úr Garðaríki.	Halldor Snorrason had been out in The-Great-City with Harald as before was said and came to Norway with him east from Gardariki.	Halldor Snorrason had been to Constantinople with Harald as has been said before, and went east to Norway with him from the Kievan Rus'.
Hafði hann þá mikla sæmd og virðing af Haraldi konungi.	Had he then much honour and worthiness from Harald the-king.	Then he had much honour and worthiness from king Harald.
Var hann með konungi þenna vetur er hann sat í Kaupangi.	Was he with the-king that winter when he stayed at Kaupang.	He was with the king that winter when he stayed a Kaupang in Skiringssal.
En er á leið veturinn og vora tók bjuggu menn kaupferðir sínar snemma því að nálega hafði engi eða lítill verið skipagangur af Noregi fyrir sakar ófriðar og aga þess sem verið hafði milli Noregs og Danmerkur.	And when had passed winter and spring took preparations people trading-voyages theirs early because of nearly had none or little been shipping from Norway for the-sake-of hostilities and turbulence those as had-been had between Norway and Denmark.	And when winter had passed into spring, people began preparations for trading voyages early, because there had been little in the way of trade from Norway because of hostilities and turbulence between Norway and Denmark.
En er á leið vorið fann Haraldur konungur að Halldór Snorrason ógladdist mjög.	But when that passed spring found Harald the-king that Halldór Snorrason un-glad much.	But when spring had passed, king Harald found Halldor Snorrason very unhappy.
Konungur spurði einn dag hvað honum bjó í skapi.	The-king asked one day what he settled in mood.	One day the king asked what had settled in his mood.
Halldór svarar:	Halldor answered:	Halldor answered:
"Út fýsir mig til Íslands herra".	"Out desire me to Iceland lord".	"I desire to travel out to Iceland, lord".
Konungur mælti:	The-king spoke:	The king said:
"Margur mundi þó heimfúsari verið hafa eða hver eru fararefni eða hversu verst fénu?"	"Many would though home-longing being had but where are travel-goods or how-so becomes wealth?"	"Many would be longing for home, but where are your travel goods, and how will you spend your wealth?"

The Tale of Halldor Snorrason II (Old Icelandic)

Old Icelandic	Literal	English
Hann svarar:	He answered:	He answered:
"Skjótt ætla eg að verja því að ekki er til nema ígangsklæði mín".	"Swift intend I to spend because that not have to take travelling-clothes mine".	"Swiftly it seems spent to me, because I don't have any travelling clothes to take".
"Lítt er þá launuð löng þjónusta og margur háski og skal eg fá þér skip og áhöfnina.	"Little is then repaid long service and many dangers and shall I pay you a-ship and crew.	"Your long service and all its dangers are little repaid, and I shall buy you a ship and a crew.
Skal faðir þinn sjá mega að þú hefir mér eigi til engis þjónað".	Shall father yours see may that you have me not to nothing served".	Your father shall see that you have not served me for nothing".
Halldór þakkaði konungi gjöfina.	Halldor thanked the-king the-gift.	Halldor thank the king for his gift.
Fám dögum síðar fann Halldór konung og spurði konungur hversu mjög hann hefði ráðið sér skipverja.	A-few days later found Halldor the-king and asked the-king how-so much he had hired for the-crew.	A few days later Halldor found the king and asked him how much of the crew had he hired.
Hann svarar:	He answered:	He answered:
"Allir kaupsveinar hafa sér ráðið áður skipan en eg fæ enga menn og því ætla eg að eftir mun verða að vera skip það er þér gáfuð mér".	"All trading-men have themselves hired other ships but I give no men and therefore suppose I that remaining should be that becoming the-ship that is you gave me".	"All the traders have been hired by other ships, but I have got no men, and therefore I suppose that the ship that you gave me should remain".
Konungur mælti:	The-king spoke:	The king spoke:
"Eigi er þá vinveitt gjöfin og skulum við enn bíða hvað úr ráðist um háseta".	"Not is then favourable gift and shall with then wait what from decide about sailors".	"Then it is not a favourable gift, and with that we shall wait to decide about the sailors".
Annan dag eftir var blásið til móts í bænum og sagt að konungur vill tala við bæjarmenn og kaupmenn.	The-next day after was trumpet-blown to meet in the-town and said that the-king wished-to speak with townspeople and merchants.	The next day the trumpet was blown to meet in the town, and the king said that he wished to speak with the townspeople and the merchants.
Konungur kom seint til mótsins og sýndist með áhyggjusvip þá er hann kom.	The-king came late to the-meeting and seemed with worried-face then as he came.	The king came late to the meeting and seemed to have a worried face when he arrived.
Hann mælti:	He spoke:	He spoke:

The Tale of Halldor Snorrason II (Old Icelandic)

Old Icelandic	Literal	English
"Það heyrum vér sagt að ófriður muni kominn í ríki vort austur í Vík.	"This hear we said that un-peace shall come in kingdom ours east about Vik.	"We hear this, that war shall come to our kingdom east in Vik.
Ræður Sveinn Danakonungur fyrir Danaher og vill oss vinna skaða en vér viljum með engu móti upp gefa vor lönd.	Leading Svein King-of-Denmark for Danish-forces and wishes us to-win-over damages but we wish-to with none meet up give our land.	King Svein of Denmark is leading the Danish forces and means to win over and damage us, but none of us wish to give up our land.
Fyrir því leggjum vér bann fyrir hvert skip að úr landi fari fyrr en eg hefi slíkt sem eg vil af hverju skipi, bæði af liði og vistum, nema einn knörr eigi mikill er á Halldór Snorrason skal ganga til Íslands.	For therefore lay we a-ban before each ship to out-of-the-land travel before that I have such as I wish from each ship, both of men and provisions, except one ship not great that of Halldor Snorrason shall go to Iceland.	Therefore we lay a ban on each ship from travelling out of these lands, until I have what I wish from each ship, men and provisions, except for one small ship of Halldor Snorrason which will go to Iceland.
En þótt yður þyki þetta nokkuð strangt er áður hafið búið ferðir yðrar þá ber oss nauðsyn til slíkra álaga en betra þætti oss að um kyrrt væri að sitja og færi hver sem vildi".	But though you think this somewhat strange is before have prepared travel yours then bears us necessity to such stress but better seems to-us that about peace was that settle and travel each as wish".	You will think this somewhat strange, when you have prepared your travel, but it this stress is necessary, and it would be better for us if there was peace and each man could travel wherever he wished.
Eftir það sleit mótinu.	After that broken-up the-meeting.	After that the meeting was broken up.
Litlu síðar kom Halldór á konungs fund.	Little afterwards came Halldor to the-king find.	A little afterwards Halldor came to find the king.
Konungur spurði hvað þá liði um búnaðinn, hvort hann fengi nokkura háseta.	The-king asked what then crew about preparations, each he found some crew.	The king asked about what preparations had been made for some crew.
Halldór svarar:	Halldor answered:	Halldor answered:
"Helsti marga hefi eg nú ráðið því að miklu fleiri koma nú til mín og beiða fars en eg megi öllum veita og veita menn mér mikinn atgang að drjúgum eru brotin hús til mín svo að hvorki nótt né dag hefi eg ró fyrir ákallsi manna hér um".	"Rather many have I now hired because that a-great more came now to me and asked travel than I may all lead and grant people me much access that greatly they violated house to me so that neither night nor day have I rest for calling people here about".	"I have hired rather a lot of men, because a great more came to me and asked to travel than I may lead, and granted much access that my house is violated, so that I have no rest, neither day nor night for these people calling here abouts".

The Tale of Halldor Snorrason II (Old Icelandic)

Old Icelandic	Literal	English
Konungur mælti:	The-king spoke:	The king spoke:
"Haltu nú þessum hásetum sem þú hefir tekið og sjáum enn hvað í gerist".	"Hold-you now those sailors that you have taken and we-see then what will be".	"Now keep the sailors that you have hired, and we will see what will happen".
Næsta dag eftir var blásið og sagt að konungur vill enn tala við kaupmenn.	Next day after was trumpet-blown and said the king wished then speak with the-merchants.	The next day, a trumpet was blown, and it was said that the king wished to speak with the merchants.
Nú var eigi sein aðkoma konungs til mótsins því að hann kom í fyrsta lagi.	Now was not late to-come the-king to the-meeting because that he came to first had.	Now the king was not late in coming to the meeting, because he had arrived first.
Var hann þá blíðlegur í yfirbragði.	Was he then happily in complexion.	He was then happy in his complexion.
Hann stóð upp og mælti:	He stood up and spoke:	He stood up and spoke:
"Nú eru góð tíðindi að segja.	"Now there-are good tidings to say.	"Now there is good news to say.
Það er ekki nema upplost og lygi er þér heyrðuð sagt um ófriðinn fyrra dag.	That is not except false-rumour and lie that you heard said about un-peace the-first day.	That was nothing except a false rumour and a lie that you heard said about war the other day.
Viljum vér nú leyfa hverju skipi úr landi að fara þangað sem hver vill sínu skipi halda.	Wish we now allow each ship out-of lands to travel from-there as each wishes their ship to-hold.	We now wish to allow each ship out of our lands to travel where they wish with their ships.
Komið aftur að hausti og færið oss gersemar.	Come back in the-autumn and bring us treasures.	Come back in the autumn, and bring us treasures.
En þér skuluð hafa af oss í mót gæði og vingan".	But you should have from us in return good-things and friendship".	Then you shall have good things and friendship in return from us".
Allir kaupmenn er þar voru urðu þessu fegnir og báðu hann tala konunga heilastan.	All the-traders who there were became this celebrated and bid him speak the-king thanks.	All the traders who were there celebrated at this and spoke thanks to the king.
Fór Halldór til Íslands um sumarið og var þann vetur með föður sínum.	Travelled Halldor to Iceland about summer and was then winter with father his.	Halldor travelled to Iceland around summer and was there with his father for the winter.

The Tale of Halldor Snorrason II (Old Icelandic)

Old Icelandic	Literal	English
Hann fór utan eftir um sumarið og þá enn til hirðar Haralds konungs og er svo sagt að Halldór var þá eigi jafnfylginn konungi sem fyrr og sat hann eftir um aftna þá er konungur gekk að sofa.	He travelled out after about summer and then was to court Harald the-king and was so said that Halldor was then not equally-following the-king as before and sat he after about evening then when the-king went to sleep.	He travelled around summer and was then in the court of king Harald, and so it was said that Halldor was not the same follower of the king that he was before, and he sat up in the evening after the king had gone to sleep.

2

Old Icelandic	Literal	English
Maður hét Þórir Englandsfari og hafði verið hinn mesti kaupmaður og lengi í siglingum til ýmissa landa og fært konungi gersemar.	A-man named Thorir England-Traveller and had been the most trading-man and long with sailing to various lands and bringing the-king treasure.	A man was named Thorir the England-Traveller, and he had been the greatest trader and had long sailed to various lands to bring the king treasure.
Þórir var hirðmaður Haralds konungs og þá mjög gamall.	Thorir was court-man Harald the-king and then much old.	Thorir was a court man of king Harald and was then very old.
Þórir kom að máli við konung og mælti:	Thorir came to speak with the-king and spoke:	Thorir came to speak with the king and said:
"Eg er maður gamall sem þér vitið og mæðist eg mjög.	"I am a-man old as you know and tired I-am much.	"I am an old man as you know, and I am very tired.
Þykist eg nú eigi til fær að fylgja hirðsiðum, minni að drekka eða um aðra hluti þá sem til heyra.	Think I now not to travel to follow king's-men-customs, mine to drink or about other things then as to hear.	I now do not think I can follow the customs of the king's men, less drinking or other things which are heard of.
Mun nú annars leita verða þótt þetta sé best og blíðast að vera með yður".	Should now another seek to-be though it is best and happiest to be with you".	I should now seek another place to be, though it is best and happiest to be with you".
Konungur svarar:	The-king answered:	The king answered:
"Þar er okkur hægt til úrræða vinur.	"There is our possible to solution friend.	"There is a possible solution, friend".
Ver með hirðinni og drekk ekki meira en þú vilt í mínu leyfi".	Be with court and drink not more than you wish with my leave".	Be with the court and do not drink more than you wish, with my leave".
Bárður hét maður upplenskur, góður drengur og ekki gamall.	Bard was-named a-man an-Upplander, good fellow and not old.	There was a man named Bard, an Upplander, a good fellow and not old.

The Tale of Halldor Snorrason II (Old Icelandic)

Old Icelandic	Literal	English
Hann var með Haraldi konungi í miklum kærleikum.	He was with Harald the-king in much dearly-loved.	He was with king Harald and much loved by him.
Voru þeir sessunautar, Bárður, Þórir og Halldór.	Were they sitting-together, Bard, Thorir and Halldor.	They were sitting together, Bard, Thorir, and Halldor.
Og eitt kveld er konungur gekk þar fyrir er þeir sátu og drukku, í því bili gaf Halldór upp hornið.	And one evening when the-king went there before were they sat and drinking, in that moment gave Halldor up the-drinking-horn.	And one evening when the king went before where they sat drinking, in that moment Halldor gave up the drinking horn.
Það var dýrshorn mikið og skyggt vel.	It was stag-horn huge and shaded well.	It was a stag horn, and very transparent.
Sá gjörla í gegnum að hann hafði drukkið vel til hálfs við Þóri	So completely in through that he had drunk well to half against Thorir	So completely through, that it could be seen that he had drunk more than half compared to Thorir
en honum gekk seint af að drekka.	who he went slowly of to drink.	who drank slowly.
Þá mælti konungur:	Then spoke the-king:	Then the king spoke:
"Seint er þó menn að reyna Halldór",	"Slow it-is though people to know Halldor",	"It is slow to get to know Halldor",
segir hann	said he	he said,
"er þú níðist á drykkju við gamalmenni og hleypur að vændiskonum um síðkveldum en fylgir eigi konungi þínum".	"that you down the drinks against old-men and run to prostitutes about late-evening while following not king yours".	"that you down the drinks against old men, and run to prostitutes late in the evening, while not following your king".
Halldór svarar engu en Bárður fann að honum mislíkaði umræða konungs.	Halldor answered none but Bard found that he misliked discussion the-king's.	Halldor did not answer, but Bard found that he disliked the king's words.
Fór Bárður þegar um myrgininn snemma á fund konungs.	Went Bard straight-away about morning early to find the-king.	Bard went straight away early in the morning to find the king.
"Þó ert þú nú árrisull Bárður",	"Though are you now early-riser Bard",	"Though you are an early riser, Bard",
segir konungur.	said the-king.	said the king.
"Em eg nú kominn",	"Am I now come",	"And I have now come",

The Tale of Halldor Snorrason II (Old Icelandic)

Old Icelandic	Literal	English
kvað Bárður,	said Bard,	said Bard,
"að ávíta yður herra.	"to warn you lord.	"to warn you lord.
Þér mæltuð illa og ómaklega í gærkveld til Halldórs vinar yðvars er þér kennduð honum að hann drykki sleitilega því að það var horn Þóris og hafði hann unnið og ætlaði að bera til skapkers ef eigi drykki Halldór fyrir hann.	You spoke ill and undeservedly about last-night to Halldor friend yours when you taught him that he drank unfairly because that it was horn Thorir's and had he deserved and intended to bear to large-vessel if not drink Halldor before him.	You spoke badly and unfairly last night to Halldor, your friend, when you told him that he drank unfairly, because it was Thorir's horn, and he deserved and intended to bear a large vessel if Halldor was not drinking before him.
Það er og hin mesta lygi er þér mæltuð að hann færi að léttlætiskonum en kjósa mundu menn að hann fylgdi þér fastara".	It is also the most lie that you spoke that he went to prostitutes than choose should people to him follow you more-fixedly".	It is also the greatest lie that you said he went to prostitutes, although people would rather that he followed you more closely".
Konungur svarar og lét að þeir mundu semja þetta mál með sér þá er þeir Halldór fyndust.	The-king answered and had that they would negotiate this matter with him then when they Halldor found.	The king answered that he would negotiate this matter with him when he met Halldor next.
Hittir Bárður Halldór og segir honum góð orð konungs til hans og kvað einsætt vera að hann léti sér einskis þykja um vert orðaframkast konungs og á Bárður hinn besta hlut að með þeim.	Found Bard Halldor and said he good words the-king's to him and said clearly being that he let himself nothing think about worthy outburst the-king's and this Bard the best part that between them.	Bard found Halldor and told him the king's good words, and that he should let himself think no worth of the king's outburst, and this is how Bard tried to put the best part between them.
Líður fram að jólum og er heldur fátt um með þeim konungi og Halldóri.	Passed from to Yule and was rather few about with them the-king and Halldor.	Time passed until Yule, and there was little between the king and Halldor.
Og er að jólum kemur þá eru víti upp sögð sem þar er tíska til.	And when that Yule came then they-were signalled up told as there was custom to.	And when Yule came, were they signalled up as was the custom.
Og einn morgun jólanna er breytt hringingum.	And one morning Yule was changed bell-ringing.	And one morning during Yule, the bell ringing was changed.

The Tale of Halldor Snorrason II (Old Icelandic)

Old Icelandic	Literal	English
Gáfu kertisveinar klokkurum fé til að hringja miklu fyrr en vant var og varð Halldór víttur og fjöldi annarra manna og settust í hálm um daginn og skyldu drekka vítin.	Gave court-men clocks payment for to ring much before than expected was and became Halldor reprimanded and many other people and sat in the-straw about the-day and should drink penalty.	The court men gave the bell ringers payment to ring the bells much before it was expected, and Halldor was reprimanded along with many other people, who had to sit on the floor in the straw and drink from the penalty horn.
Halldór situr í rúmi sínu og færa þeir honum eigi að síður vítið en hann lést eigi drekka mundu.	Halldor sat in seat his and brought they him none the less the-penalty and he had not drank would.	Halldor sat in his room, and they none the less brought him the penalty horn, and he would not drink from it.
Þeir segja þá konungi til.	They told then the-king about.	They told the king about it.
"Það mun eigi satt",	"That could not be-true",	"That could not be true",
segir konungur, "og mun hann við taka ef eg færi honum",	said the-king, "and should he with take if I bring him",	said the king,
tekur síðan vítishornið og gengur að Halldóri.	took then penalty-horn and went to Halldor.	"and he should take it if I bring it to him", and he took the penalty horn and went to Halldor.
Hann stendur upp í móti honum.	He stood up in meeting him.	He stood up upon meeting him.
Konungur biður hann drekka vítið.	The-king asked him to-drink the-penalty.	The king asked him to drink the penalty.
Halldór svarar:	Halldor answered:	Halldor answered:
"Eg þykist ekki víttur að heldur þó að þér setjið brögð til hringinga til þess eins að gera mönnum víti".	"I think not penalty to hold though that you set a-trick to bell-ringing to this alone to do people punishment".	"I don't think to hold the penalty, though you set a trick to the bell ringing only to punish people".
Konungur svarar:	The-king answered:	The king answered:
"Þú munt drekka skulu vítið þó eigi síður en aðrir menn".	"You must drink should penalty though not less than other people".	"You must drink the penalty no less than other people".
"Vera má það konungur",	"Be may that king",	"That may be, king",
segir Halldór,	said Halldor,	said Halldor,

The Tale of Halldor Snorrason II (Old Icelandic)

Old Icelandic	Literal	English
"að þú komir því á leið að eg drekki.	"that you come with to pass that I drink.	"that it shall come to pass that I drink.
En það kann eg þó segja þér að eigi mundi Sigurður sýr fá nauðgað Snorra goða til"	But that know I though say to-you that not would Sigurd Sow gave force Snorri the-priest to",	But I know to say to you that Sigurd Sow would not have forced Snorri the Priest to",
og vill seilast til hornsins sem hann gerir og drekkur af en konungur reiðist mjög og gengur til rúms síns.	and willed to-reach for the-horn as he went and drank of as the-king commanded much and went to room his.	and he reached for the penalty horn, and drank as much as the king commanded, and went to his room.
Og er kemur hinn átti dagur jóla var mönnum gefinn máli.	And when came the eighth day Yule were people given payment.	And when the eighth day of Yule came, people were given payment.
Það var kallað Haraldsslátta.	That was called Harald's-money.	That was called Harald's money.
Var meiri hlutur kopars, það besta kosti að væri helmings silfur.	Was greater part copper, that best benefit that had half silver.	It was for the greater part copper, and the best of it was half silver.
Og er Halldór tók málann hefir hann í möttulsskauti sínu silfrið og lítur á og sýnist eigi skírt málasilfrið, lýstur undir neðan annarri hendi og fer það allt í hálm niður.	And when Halldor took payment had he in cloak-lap his the-silver and looked at and seemed not pure silverware, struck under below other hand and went it all in straw below.	And when Halldor took the payment, he put the silver in the lap of his cloak, and it seemed not to be pure silver, he swept it down with his other hand and it all went onto the straw on the floor below.
Bárður mælti, kvað hann illa með fara:	Bard spoke, said he badly with went:	Bard spoke, and said that he was behaving badly:
"Mun konungur þykjast svívirður í og leitað á við hann um málagjöfina".	"Would the-king consider dishonourable of and consider to with him about payment".	"The king would consider this dishonourable, considering with him about payment".
"Ekki má nú fara að slíku",	"Not may now go that such",	"It may not go that way",
segir Halldór,	said Halldor,	said Halldor,
"litlu hættir nú til".	"little way now to".	"there is little to be done now".

3

Nú er frá því sagt að þeir búa skip sín eftir jólin.	Now was from of said that they prepared ships theirs after Yule.	Now it was said that they prepared their ships after Yule.

The Tale of Halldor Snorrason II (Old Icelandic)

Old Icelandic	Literal	English
Ætlar konungur suður fyrir land.	Intended the-king south along the-land.	The king intended to travel south along the land.
Og er konungur var mjög svo búinn þá bjóst Halldór ekki og mælti Bárður:	And when the-king was much so prepared then readied Halldor not and spoke Bard:	And when the king was so well prepared, Halldor did not prepare, and Bard said,
"Hví býstu eigi Halldór?"	"Why prepared not Halldor?"	"Why do you not prepare Halldor?"
"Eigi vil eg",	"Not wish I",	"I do not want to,"
segir hann,	said he,	he said,
"og ekki ætla eg að fara.	"and not intend I to travel.	"and I do not intend to travel.
Sé eg nú að konungur þokkar ekki mitt mál".	See I now that the-king favours not my measure".	I see now that the king does not like my case".
Bárður segir:	Bard said:	Bard said:
"Hann mun þó að vísu vilja að þú farir".	"He would though that certainly wish that you travel".	"Though he will want you to travel".
Fer Bárður síðan og hittir konung, segir honum að Halldór býst ekki:	Went Bard afterwards and found the-king, said he that Halldor prepares not	Afterwards Bad went and found the king, and he told him that Halldor had not prepared,
"Máttu svo ætla að vandskipaður mun þér vera stafninn í stað hans".	"May-you so suppose that difficult would you be the-prow in replace his".	"you may suppose that it would be difficult to replace him in the prow of the ship".
Konungur mælti:	The-king spoke:	The king spoke:
"Seg honum að eg ætla að hann skuli mér fylgja og þetta er ekki alugað, fæð sjá er með okkur er um hríð".	"Say to-him that I intend that he shall with-me follow and this is not resolved, sadness see that with us is about awhile".	"Tell him that I intend that he shall follow with me, and this is not resolved, this sadness that has been seen between us for a while".
Bárður hittir Halldór og lætur að konungur vilji einskis kostar láta hans þjónustu og það ræðst úr að Halldór fer og halda þeir konungur suður með landi.	Bard found Halldor and leave that the-king willed no choice losing his service and that commanded from that Halldor went and held they the-king south along the-land.	Bard found Halldor and put to him that the king gave no choice to lose his service, and that it was a command, and from that Halldor went and they held with the king south along the land.

The Tale of Halldor Snorrason II (Old Icelandic)

Old Icelandic	Literal	English
Og einhverja nótt er þeir sigldu þá mælti Halldór til þess er stýrði:	And one-such night that they sailed then spoke Halldor to that who steered:	And on one such night the sailed, Halldor spoke to the steersman,
"Lát ýkva",	"Let-it veer",	"let it veer",
segir hann.	said he.	he said.
Konungur mælti til stýrimanns:	The-king spoke to the-steersman:	The king spoke to the steersman,
"Halt svo fram", segir hann.	"Hold so forwards", said he.	"hold straight on", he said.
Halldór mælti öðru sinni:	Halldor spoke a-second his:	Halldor spoke a second time:
"Lát ýkva".	"Let-it veer".	"Let it veer".
Konungur segir enn á sömu leið.	The-king said then of the-same way.	The king said the same way.
Halldór mælti:	Halldor spoke:	Halldor spoke:
"Beint stefnið þér skerið".	"Direction heading you-to a-rock".	"You are heading directly for a rock".
Og að því varð þeim.	And that accordingly became of-them.	And so it happened of them.
Því næst gekk undan skipinu undirhluturinn og varð þá að flytja til lands með öðrum skipum og síðan var skotið landtjald og bætt að skipinu.	Because next went under the-ship the-under-part and became then that carried to land with other ships and afterwards were launched land-tents and repaired the ship.	Because next the underneath of the ship went and it then had to be carried to the land with other ships, and then a land tent was set up, and they ship was repaired.
Við það vaknar Bárður er Halldór bindur húðfat sitt.	With that awoke Bard that Halldor tied-up hammock his.	With that Bard awoke to find Halldor tying up his hammock.
Bárður spyr hvað hann ætlist fyrir.	Bard asked what he intended for.	Bard asked what his intention was.
En Halldór kvaðst ætla á byrðing er lá skammt frá þeim	Then Halldor said intend to merchant-ship that lay short-distance from them	Then Halldor said that he intended to go to a merchant ship that lay a short distance from them,

The Tale of Halldor Snorrason II (Old Icelandic)

Old Icelandic	Literal	English
"og kann vera að nú leggi sundur reyki vora og er þetta fullreynt.	"and can it-be that now lay separate smoke going and is that fully-tested.	"and it may be that now our smoke is falling apart, and it has been fully tried".
Og eigi vil eg að konungur spilli oftar skipum sínum eða öðrum gersemum mér til svívirðingar og að mér beri þá verr en áður".	And not wish I the king spoil more-often ships his or other treasure me to disgrace and that me bear then worse than before".	And I do not want the king to spoil his ships or other treasures more often to disgrace me, and treat me then worse than before".
"Bíð enn",	"Wait still",	"Still, wait",
segir Bárður,	said Bard,	said Bard,
"eg vil enn hitta konung".	"I will but find the-king".	"I will just find the king".
Og er hann kemur mælti konungur:	And when he came spoke-to the-king:	And when he came the king spoke:
"Snemma ertu á fótum Bárður".	"Soon are-you about feed Bard".	"You are early on your feet, Bard".
"Svo er nú þörf herra.	"So is now needed lord.	"So it is needed now, lord.
Halldór er í brautbúnaði og þykir þú óvingjarnlega til sín gert hafa og er nokkuð vant að gæta til með ykkur.	Halldor is to away-prepared and thinks you unfriendly to him done have and is something difficult that take-care to with you-two.	Halldor is preparing to go away and thinks that you have been unfriendly towards him, and it's difficult to keep the peace between you two.
Ætlar hann nú í brott og ráðast til skips og fara út til Íslands með reiði og fer þá ómaklega ykkar skilnaður.	Intends he now to away and appoint to a-ship and travel out to Iceland with anger and goes then undeservedly with-you parting.	He now intends to go away and join a ship and travel to Iceland in anger, and that's not a proper way for you to part.
Og það hygg eg að varla fáir þú þér annan mann jafntraustan honum".	And it think I that hardly few you to-you another man equally-trustworthy as-him".	And I think that you will hardly find another man as equally trustworthy as him".
Konungur lét að þeir mundu enn sættast og kvað sér ekki mundu að þessu þykja.	The-king had it they would still reconcile and said himself not would of this think.	The king said that they would still reconcile and said he would not think about it.
Bárður hittir Halldór og segir honum vingjarnleg orð konungs.	Bard found Halldor and told him friendly words the-king's.	Bard found Halldor and told him the king's friendly words.
Halldór svarar:	Halldor answered:	Halldor answered:

The Tale of Halldor Snorrason II (Old Icelandic)

Old Icelandic	Literal	English
"Til hvers skal eg honum þjóna lengur? Þatgi að eg fái mála minn falslaust".	"To how shall I him serve longer? That-not that I get matter mine without-fraud".	"Why should I serve him any longer? Let me have my case without fraud".
Bárður mælti:	Bard spoke:	Bard said,
"Get eigi þess.	"Get not like-this.	"Don't talk like this.
Vel máttu þér það líka láta er lendra manna synir hafa og ekki fórstu að því með vægð næsta sinni er þú slóst niður í hálm silfrinu og ónýttir.	Well may you that like allow what is-paid people sons have and not went-you that therefore with grace next-to yourself when you struck down into the-straw the-silver and un-used.	Well, you might as well have what the sons of the land have, and you did not do it mercifully the next time you struck the silver down in the straw and wasted it.
Og máttu víst vita að konungi þykir það svívirðlega til sín gert".	And may certainly know that the-king thought that dishonourable to him done".	And you must know that the king considers it disgraceful to do so".
Halldór svarar:	Halldor answered:	Halldor answered:
"Eigi má eg það vita að neitt sinn hafi jafnmjög logist í um fylgdina mína sem í málagjöfina konungs".	"Not may I that certainly that nothing he has equally-much cheated in about following mine as in payment the-king's".	"I do not know of having cheated him in my following as much as he has cheated me with the king's payment".
"Satt mun það vera",	"True would that be",	"That may be true",
segir Bárður,	said Bard,	said Bard,
"biðleika, enn vil eg hitta konung".	"wait, then will I find the-king".	"wait, then I will find the king".
Og svo gerði hann.	And so did he.	And he did so.
Og er Bárður hitti konung mælti hann:	And when Bard found the-king spoke he:	And when Bard found the king, he spoke:
"Fá Halldóri mála sinn skíran því að verður er hann að hafa".	"Get Halldor payment his cleared because that worth is he to have".	"Get Halldor his payment cleared, because he is worth having".
Konungur svarar:	The-king answered:	The king answered:

The Tale of Halldor Snorrason II (Old Icelandic)

Old Icelandic	Literal	English
"Líst þér eigi nokkur svo djörfung í að krefja Halldóri annars mála en taka lendra manna synir og með slíkri svívirðing sem hann fór með málanum næstum?"	"Appears to-you not something so bold that to demand Halldor another payment than take payment people's sons and with such disgrace as he did with payment before?"	"Does it not appear you you somewhat bold to demand Halldor a payment other than people's sons, and with such disgrace as he did with his last payment?"
Bárður svarar:	Bard answered:	Bard answered:
"Á hitt er að líta herra er miklu er meira vert, drengskap hans og vináttu ykkra er lengi hefir góð verið og þar með stórmennsku þína.	"To find that to look lord that much is more worth, honour his and friendship yours that long has good been and there with greatness yours.	"The other thing is to look, lord, at who is much more valuable, his boyhood and your friendship that has been good for a long time and thus your greatness.
Og veistu skap Halldórs og stirðlæti og er það þinn vegur að gera honum sóma".	And know-you mood Halldor's and hard-temper and that it your way that to-do him honour".	And we know Halldór's mood and stiffness, and it's your way to do him honor".
Konungur mælti:	The-king spoke:	The king said:
"Fáið honum silfrið".	"Give him the-silver".	"Give him the silver".
Var nú svo gert.	Was now so done.	Now this was done.
Kemur Bárður til Halldórs og færir honum tólf aura brennda og mælti:	Came Bard to Halldor and brought him twelve ounces burnt and spoke:	Bard came to Halldor and brought him twelve ounces of refined silver and spoke:
"Sérð þú eigi að þú hefir slíkt er þú brekar af konungi og hann vill að þú hafir slíkt af honum sem þú þykist þurfa?"	"See you not that you have such that you keep-asking of the-king and he wishes that you have such of him as you think you-need?"	"Do you not see that you ask of the king, and he wishes to to have what you think you need, if only you ask for it?"
Halldór svarar:	Halldor answered:	Halldor answeed:
"Eigi skal eg þó oftar vera á konungsskipinu og ef hann vill hafa mitt föruneyti lengur þá vil eg hafa skip til stjórnar og eignast það".	"Not shall I though frequent be in the-king's-ship and if he wishes to-have my companionship longer then wish I to-have ship to steer and own it".	"I shall not be on the king's ship more often, and if he wishes to have me in his company any longer, then I wish to have my own ship to steer".
Bárður svarar:	Bard answered:	Bard answered:

The Tale of Halldor Snorrason II (Old Icelandic)

Old Icelandic	Literal	English
"Það samir eigi að lendir menn láti skip sín fyrir þér og ertu of framgjarn".	"It so not to landed men have ships theirs for you and are-you over ambitious".	"It is not so that landed man give up their ships for you, and you are over-ambitious".
Halldór kvaðst eigi fara mundu ellegar.	Halldor said not travelling would otherwise.	Halldor said that he would not travel otherwise.
Bárður segir konungi hvers beitt er af Halldórs hendi	Bard told the-king what asked had of Halldor's hand	Bard told the king what Halldor had asked for
"og ef hásetar þess skips eru jafntraustir sem stýrimaður þá mun vel hlýða".	"and if sailors these ships were equally-trustworthy as steersman then would well listen-to".	"and if the sailors of these ships were equally trustworthy as the steersman then they would listen to him well".
Konungur mælti:	The-king spoke:	The king said,
"Þótt þetta þyki framarla mælt vera þá skal þó af nakkvað gera".	"Though this think forward spoken is then shall though of something do".	"Though this be thought to be far-fetched, something must be done".
Sveinn úr Lyrgju, lendur maður, stýrði skipi.	Fellow from Lyrgja, land man, steered a-ship.	Svein from Lyrgja, a landed man, steered a ship.
Konungur lét hann kalla á mál við sig.	The-king had him called and conversed with him.	The king had him called and discussed with him.
"Þannug er farið",	"That-way is travelled",	"It is so",
segir konungur,	said the-king,	said the king,
"sem þú veist að þú ert maður stórættaður.	"that you know that you are a-man of-high-family.	"that you know that you are a man of great family.
Vil eg fyrir því að þú sért á mínu skipi en eg mun þar fá annan mann til skipstjórnar.	Wish I for therefore that you be on my ship but I should there get another man to ship-steer.	I want you to be on my ship, but I will get another man to captain it.
Þú ert maður viskur og vil eg einkum hafa þig við ráð mín".	You are a-man wise and wish I especially have you with advise me".	You are a man of wisdom and I especially want you with my advice".
Hann segir:	He said:	He said:
"Meir hefir þú aðra menn haft við þínar ráðagerðir hér til og til þess em eg lítt fær eða hverjum er þá skipið ætlað?"	"More have you other men had with you advice-giving here to and to this am I little accomplished but who is then ship intended?"	"You have had other men with your advice so far and to the point that I can do little, but who is the ship intended for?"

64

The Tale of Halldor Snorrason II (Old Icelandic)

Old Icelandic	Literal	English
"Halldór Snorrason skal hafa",	"Halldor Snorrason shall have",	"Halldor Snorrason shall have it",
segir konungur.	said the-king.	said the king.
Sveinn segir:	The-fellow said:	Sveinn said:
"Eigi kom mér það í hug að þú mundir íslenskan mann til þess velja en taka mig frá skipstjórn".	"Not came to-me that to think that you would Icelander man to this will then take me from ship-steering".	"It never occurred to me that you would choose an Icelander for that, still take me from the captaincy".
Konungur mælti:	The-king spoke:	The king said,
"Hans ætt er eigi verri á Íslandi en þín hér í Noregi og eigi hefir enn alllangt síðan liðið er þeir voru norrænir er nú byggja Ísland".	"His ancestry is not worse as Icelander but your forces in Norway and not has-been but all-long since passed that they were Norwegians that now settle Iceland".	"His family is no worse in Iceland than yours here in Norway, and it has not been long since they were Norwegians who now inhabit Iceland".
Nú fer það fram sem konungur vill að Halldór tekur við skipi og fóru síðan austur til Óslóar, tóku þar veislur.	Now went that from as the-king wished that Halldor took with ship and travelled afterwards east to Oslo, took there feasts.	Now it went as the king wished, that Halldor took the ship, and travelled afterwards east to Oslo, where they took to feasting.

4

Það er sagt einnhvern dag er þeir konungur sátu við drykkju og var Halldór þar í konungsstofunni að sveinar hans komu þar, þeir er skipið skyldu varðveita, og voru allir votir og sögðu að þeir Sveinn höfðu tekið skipið en rekið þá á kaf.	It was said one-such day that there the-king sat with drinking and was Halldor there in the-king's-chambers the fellows his came there, they were ship should guard-over, and were all wet and said that they Svein had taken the-ship and thrown them to overboard.	It was said that one day the king and Halldor sat drinking in the king's chambers, and in came the men who were watching over his ship came in, and they were all wet, and they said that Svein had taken the ship and thrown them overboard.
Halldór stóð upp og gekk fyrir konung og spurði hvort hann skyldi eiga skipið og haldast það er konungur hafði mælt.	Halldor stood up and went before the-king and asked how he should own the-ship and hold that which the-king had spoken-of.	Halldor stood up and went before the king and asked whether he would own the ship as the king had promised.

The Tale of Halldor Snorrason II (Old Icelandic)

Old Icelandic	Literal	English
Konungur svarar og kvað það að vísu haldast skyldu, kvaddi til síðan hirðina að þeir skyldu taka sex skip og fara með Halldóri og hafa þrenna skipun á hverju.	The-king answered and said that it certainly hold should, called to since guardsmen that they should take six ships and travel with Halldor and have treble crew on each.	The king answered and said that he would keep his promise, and then called to the guardsmen that they should take six ships, travelling with a treble crew on each.
Þeir snúa nú eftir þeim Sveini og lætur hann eltast að landi og þegar hljóp Sveinn á land upp en þeir Halldór tóku skipið og fóru til konungs.	They turned now after they Svein and let he chased to land and there ran Svein on-the land up and there Halldor took the-ship and went to the-king.	They now turned after Svein and gave him chase ashore, and there Svein ran ashore, but Halldor took the ship and went to the king.
Og er veislum var lokið fer konungur norður með landi og til Þrándheims er á líður sumarið.	And when the-feasts were ended went the-king north along the-land and to Trondheim where then passed summer.	And when the feasts were over, the king went north along the land, and to Trondheim, when the summer had passed.
Sveinn úr Lyrgju sendi orð konungi að hann vill gefa upp allt málið og leggja á konungs vald að hann skipi með þeim Halldóri sem hann vill og vildi þó helst kaupa skipið ef konungi líkaði.	Svein from Lyrgja sent word to-the-king that he wished to-give up all matter and grant to the-king power that he ship with them Halldor as he wished and wished though rather purchase the-ship if the-king liked.	Svein of Lyrgja sent word to the king that he wished to give up the whole matter and put it in the king's power, that the ship would be with Halldor as he wished, but would prefer to purchase the ship if it was to the king's liking.
Og nú er konungur sér það að Sveinn skýtur öllu máli undir hans dóm þá vill hann nú svo til bregða er báðum mætti líka, falar skipið að Halldóri og vill að hann hafi verð sæmilegt en Sveinn hafi skip og kaupir konungur skip og á Halldór við hann um verð og gelst allt upp nema hálf mörk gulls stendur eftir.	And now as the-king saw that of Svein launched all matter under his deeming then wished he now so to foreclose that both may like, bargain ship that Halldor and wished that he had worth the-same that Svein had ship and bought the-king the-ship and that Halldor with him about worth and paid all up except half a-mark gold stood behind.	And now the king saw that Svein gave the whole matter up to his judgement, that he now wished to settle the matter to the liking of both parties. The ship was purchased from Halldor and he wished that he had a price the same worth as Svein to have the ship, and the king bought the ship from Halldor, and with him was the price and gold all paid except for half a gold mark left behind.
Heimtir Halldór lítt enda galst það ekki og fer svo fram um veturinn.	Got Halldor little end payment that not and went so forward about winter.	Halldor did not demand the closure of the payment, and so things went on over the winter.

The Tale of Halldor Snorrason II (Old Icelandic)

Old Icelandic	Literal	English
Og er vora tók segir Halldór konungi að hann vill til Íslands um sumarið og kvað sér vel koma að þá gyldist það sem eftir var skipverðsins.	And as spring took said Halldor to-the-king that he wished to Iceland about summer and said he well come that then repay that which remained was ship's-worth.	And as spring came, Halldor said to the king that he wished to travel to Iceland in the summer, and it would be well if he could repay the remainder of the ship's worth.
En konungur fer heldur undan um gjaldið og þykir ekki betur er hann heimtir en ekki bannar hann Halldóri útferð og býr hann skip sitt um vorið í ánni Nið og leggur út síðan við Bröttueyri.	But the-king went rather from-under about the-payment and seemed not better that he got then not ban him Halldor out-travelling and prepared he ship his about spring in the-river Nid and laid out afterwards with Bratteyar.	But the king escaped the payment, and thought not better that he demanded, but did not ban Halldor from travelling, and he prepared his ship around spring in the river Nid, nd laid out afterwards at Bratteyar.
Og er þeir voru albúnir og byrvænlegt var þá gengur Halldór upp í bæinn með nokkura menn síð um aftan.	And when they were all-prepared and promising-wind were then going Halldor up out-of town with some men later about evening.	And then they were all prepared and with a promising wind, then Halldor went up in the town with some men later in the evening.
Hann var með vopnum.	He was with weapons.	He was armed with weapons.
Gengu þar til er þau konungur og drottning sváfu.	Went they to where then the-king and the-queen slept.	They then went to where the king and queen slept.
Förunautar hans stóðu úti undir loftinu en hann gengur inn með vopnum sínum og verður glymur og skark af honum og vakna þau konungur við og spyr konungur hver þar brjótist að þeim um nætur.	Companions his stood outside under the-air then he went inside with weapons his and came echo and noise of him and awoke then the-king with and asked the-king who there breaking in-on them about night.	His companions stood outside, and he went inside and made a noise with his weapons which echoed and woke the king, who asked who was breaking in on them in the night.
"Hér er Halldór kominn og búinn til hafs og kominn á byr og er nú ráð að gjalda féið".	"Here is Halldor come and prepared to sea and coming is fair-wind and is now the-matter to pay wealth".	"Halldor is here, prepared to go to sea, and a fair wind is coming, and now is the matter to settle the payment".
"Ekki má það nú svo skjótt",	"Not may that now so swiftly",	"Now that may not be done so swiftly",
segir konungur,	said the-king,	said the king,
"og munum vér greiða fé á morgun".	"and should we assist payment in the-morning".	"and we shall assist with the payment in the morning".

The Tale of Halldor Snorrason II (Old Icelandic)

Old Icelandic	Literal	English
"Nú vil eg þegar hafa",	"Now wish I straightaway have",	"Now I wish to have it straight away",
segir Halldór,	said Halldor,	said Halldor,
"og munkat eg nú erindlaust fara.	"and shall I now errand-without go.	"and I shall not go without it.
Kann eg og skap þitt og veit eg hversu þér mun líka þessi för mín og fjárheimta hvegi sem þú lætur nú.	Know I also mood yours and know I how-so you shall like this going mine and money-insisting which as you behave now.	I also know your mood, and I know how you would like me to go, and am demanding the money which you will leave now.
Mun eg lítt trúa þér héðan frá enda er ósýnt að við finnumst svo vilgis oft að mitt sé vænna og skal nú neyta þess og sé eg að drottning hefir hring á hendi því hófi mikinn.	Shall I little believe you hence from conclude as unseen that with found so very often that mine so expected and shall now use this and see I that the-queen has a-ring on hand therefore modest greatly.	I shall not trust you again from now on, it is not clear how often we find that I have the advantage, so I shall now take advantage of this, and I see that the queen has a ring on her hand, which is accordingly greatly modest.
Fá mér þann".	Give me it".	Give it to me".
Konungur svarar:	The-king answered:	The king answered:
"Þá verðum við fara eftir skálum og vega hringinn".	"Then worth with going after bowl and weigh the-ring".	"Then it is worth going after the bowls and weighing the ring".
"Ekki þarf þess",	"Not needed is-this",	"That is not needed",
segir Halldór,	said Halldor,	said Halldor,
"tek eg hann fyrir hlut minn enda muntu nú ekki prettunum við koma að sinni og sel fram títt".	"take I it for share mine and should now not trick with coming this time and flip forward immediately".	"I will take it for my share, and you shall not try and trick me this time, and give it forward immediately".
Drottning mælti:	The-queen spoke:	The queen spoke:
		"Give him the ring, as he asks".
"Sérð þú eigi",	"See you not",	"Do you not see",
segir hún,	said she,	she said,

The Tale of Halldor Snorrason II (Old Icelandic)

Old Icelandic	Literal	English
"að hann stendur yfir þér uppi með víghug?"	"that he stands over you up with killing-mind?"	"that he stands over you with a mind to kill?"
Tekur síðan hringinn og fær Halldóri.	Took then the-ring and brought Halldor.	She then took the ring and brought it to Halldor.
Hann tekur við og þakkar þeim báðum gjaldið og biður þau vel lifa	He took with and thanked them both payment and bid them well life	He took it and thanked them both for the payment and bid them a good life
"og munum vér nú skilja".	"and shall we now separate".	"and we shall now separate".
Gengur nú út og mælti við förunauta sína, biður þá hlaupa sem tíðast til skipsins	Went now out and spoke with companions his, asked them to-run as swiftly to ship	He now went out and spoke with his companions, asking them to run swiftly to the ship
"því að ófús em eg að dveljast lengi í bænum".	"because that unwilling am I to stay long in this-town".	because I am not willing to stay long in this town.
Þeir gera svo, koma á skipið og þegar vinda sumir upp segl, sumir eru að báti, sumir heimta upp akkeri og bergst hver sem má.	They did so, came to the-ship and straightaway wind some upped the-sails, some were at the-tow-boat, some drew up the-anchor and best each as may.	They did so, and came to the ship and straight away wind came and they upped the sails, some were at the tow boat, and some drew up the anchor, each doing the best they could.
Og er þeir sigldu út skorti eigi hornblástur í bænum og það sáu þeir síðast að þrjú langskip voru á floti og lögðu eftir þeim en þó ber þá undan og í haf.	And when they sailed out shortly one horn-blast from the-city and this saw they the-last that three longships were in floating and laid after them but though carried then under and to sea.	And shortly after they had sailed out, there was a horn blast from the city, and the last thing they saw were three longships floating and laid after them, though then they were carried out to sea.
Skilur þar með þeim og byrjaði Halldóri vel út til Íslands en konungsmenn hurfu aftur er þeir sáu er Halldór bar undan og í haf út.	Separated there with them and began Halldor well out to Iceland but the-kings-men disappeared after when they saw that Halldor bore away-from and to sea out-of.	They separated with them there and Halldor started well out to Iceland, but the king's men turned bak when they saw that Halldor was carried away out to sea.

5

Halldór Snorrason var mikill maður vexti og fríður sýnum, allra manna styrkastur og vopndjarfastur.	Halldor Snorrason was a-great man well-built and handsome in-appearance, of-all men strongest and weapons-bold.	Halldor Snorrason was a great man, well built, and handsome in appearance, the strongest of all men, and the best with weapons.

The Tale of Halldor Snorrason II (Old Icelandic)

Old Icelandic	Literal	English
Það vitni bar Haraldur konungur Halldóri að hann hefði verið með honum allra manna svo að síst brygði við voveiflega hluti hvort sem að höndum bar mannháska eða fagnaðartíðindi þá var hann hvorki að glaðari né óglaðari.	That testimony gave Harald the-king Halldor that he had been with him all men so that least reacted with unexpected part which was at hand bringing human-danger or good-news then was he neither to gladness nor un-gladness.	King Harald gave a testimony of Halldor that of all the men he had been with, that he reacted least to an unexpected lot, which with hand carried danger or good news, he was neither happy nor unhappy.
Eigi neytti hann matar eða drakk eða svaf meira né minna en vandi hans var til hvort sem hann mætti blíðu eða stríðu.	Not consumed he food or drank or slept more nor less than custom his was to each as he might joyful or stressful.	He did not eat or drink or sleep more not less than his custom, whether he was happy or stressful.
Halldór var maður fámæltur, stuttorður, bermæltur, stygglyndur og ómjúkur, kappgjarn í öllum hlutum við hvern sem hann átti um.	Halldor was a-man of-few-words, short-worded, outspoken, quick-tempered and un-bending, self-willed in all things against which as he had about.	Halldor was a man of few words, short, outspoken, quick tempered and ungiving, self-willed about everything that he had.
En það kom illa við Harald konung er hann hafði nóga aðra þjónustumenn.	But this came ill with Harald the-king as he had enough other servants.	But this came badly against king Harald as he had enough other servants.
Komu þeir því lítt lyndi saman síðan Haraldur varð konungur í Noregi.	Came they therefore little temper together since Harald was king of Norway.	They did not get along well since Haraldur became king of Norway.
En er Halldór kom til Íslands gerði hann bú í Hjarðarholti.	But when Halldor came to Iceland did he settle at Hjardarholt.	But when Halldór came to Iceland he made an estate in Hjarðarholt.
Nokkurum sumrum síðar sendi Haraldur konungur orð Halldóri Snorrasyni að hann skyldi ráðast enn til hans og lét að eigi skyldi verið hafa hans virðing meiri en þá ef hann vildi farið hafa og engan mann skyldi hann hærra setja í Noregi ótiginn ef hann vildi þetta boð þekkjast.	Some summers later sent Harald the-king word-to Halldor Snorrason that he should arrange then to him and had that not should be having his honour more than then if he willed travel to-sea and only man should he highest sit in Norway un-high-born if he wished this invitation accept.	A few summers later, King Harald sent word to Halldor Snorrason that he should appoint him again, and put that his respect would not be greater than that if he wished to travel to sea, and that no man should sit higher than him in Norway if he wished to accept this invitation.
Halldór svarar svo er honum komu þessi orð:	Halldor answered so as to-him came these words:	Halldor answered when these words came to him:
"Ekki mun eg fara á fund Haralds konungs héðan af.	"Not should I travel to meet Harald the-king from-here of.	"I will not go to King Harald from now on.

The Tale of Halldor Snorrason II (Old Icelandic)

Old Icelandic	Literal	English
Mun nú hafa hvor okkar það sem fengið hefir.	Should now have each ours that which got we-have.	Each of us will now have what he has received.
Mér er kunnigt skaplyndi hans.	To-me it-is known mood-temper his.	His mood is known to me.
Veit eg gjörla að hann mundi það efna sem hann hét að setja engan mann hærra í Noregi en mig ef eg kæmi á hans fund því að hann mundi mig láta festa á hinn hæsta gálga ef hann mætti ráða".	Know I completely that he should that carry-out which he promised to sit no man higher in Norway but me if I come to him to-meet therefore that he should me have fasten to the highest gallows if he might prevail".	I know very well that he would do what he promised to put no man higher in Norway than me if I came to meet him, for he would have me fastened to the highest gallows if he could rule it".
Og er á leið mjög ævi Haralds konungs þá er sagt að hann sendi Halldóri orð til að hann skyldi senda honum melrakkabelgi, vildi gera láta af þeim yfir rekkju sína því að konungur þóttist þá þurfa hlýs.	And when had passed much age Harald the-king then that is-said that he sent Halldor word to that he should send him arctic-fox-furs, wished get have of them over bed his because that the-king thought then needed warmth.	And when king Harald became much passed with age, it is said that he sent word to Halldor that he should send him arctic fox furs, he wanted to let them go over his bed because the king thought he needed warmth.
Og er Halldóri kom sjá orðsending konungs þá er sagt að hann skyti því orði við í fyrstu:	And as Halldor came so word-sending the-king then was said that he shot accordingly word against at first:	And when Halldor came to see the king's message, it is said that he replied first:
"Eldist árgalinn nú",	"Old-is the-cockerel now",	"The yearling is getting old now",
sagði hann en sendi honum belgi.	said he but sent him furs.	he said, but sent him arctic fox furs.
En ekki fundust þeir sjálfir síðan er þeir skildust í Þrándheimi þó að þá yrði nokkuð með stytti því sinni.	But not met they themselves afterwards that the separated at Trondheim though that then became somewhat with short of themselves.	But they did not meet each other since they had separated at Trondheim, though they had taken short leave with each other.
Bjó hann í Hjarðarholti til elli og varð maður gamall.	Farmed he in Hjardarholt until old-age and became a-man old.	He lived in Hjarðarholt until old age and became an old man.

Word List (Old Icelandic to English)

Old Icelandic	English

A, a

að	at, in, in-on, it, of, that, the, this, to
aðkoma	to-come
aðra	other
aðrir	other
af	from, from, of, of
aftan	evening
aftna	evening
aftur	after, back
aga	turbulence
akkeri	the-anchor
albúnir	all-prepared
allir	all, all
alllangt	all-long
allra	all, of-all
allt	all, all
alugað	resolved
annan	another, another, the-next
annarra	other
annarri	other
annars	another, another
atgang	access
aura	ounces
austan	east
austur	east, east

Á, á

á	about, and, as, at, had, in, is, of, on, on-the, that, the, then, this, to
áður	before, other
áhöfnina	crew
áhyggjusvip	worried-face
ákallsi	calling
álaga	stress
ánni	the-river
árgalinn	the-cockerel
árrisull	early-riser
átti	eighth, had
ávíta	warn

Æ, æ

ætla	intend, suppose
ætlað	intended
ætlaði	intended
ætlar	intended, intends
ætlist	intended
ætt	ancestry
ævi	age

B, b

báðu	bid
báðum	both
bæði	both
bæinn	town
bæjarmenn	townspeople
bænum	the-city, the-town, this-town
bætt	repaired
bann	a-ban
bannar	ban
bar	bore, bringing, gave
Bárður	Bard (name)
báti	the-tow-boat
beiða	asked
beint	direction
beitt	asked
belgi	furs
ber	bears, carried
bera	bear
bergst	best
beri	bear
bermæltur	outspoken
best	best
besta	best
betra	better

Word List (Old Icelandic to English)

Old Icelandic	English
betur	better
bíð	wait
bíða	wait
biðleika	wait
biður	asked, bid
bili	moment
bindur	tied-up
bjó	farmed, settled
bjóst	readied
bjuggu	preparations
blásið	trumpet-blown
blíðast	happiest
blíðlegur	happily
blíðu	joyful
boð	invitation
brautbúnaði	away-prepared
bregða	foreclose
brekar	keep-asking
brennda	burnt
breytt	changed
brjótist	breaking
brögð	a-trick
brotin	violated
brott	away
Bröttueyri	Bratteyar (place)
brygði	reacted
bú	settle
búa	prepared
búið	prepared
búinn	prepared
búnaðinn	preparations
byggja	settle
byr	fair-wind
býr	prepared
byrðing	merchant-ship
byrjaði	began
byrvænlegt	promising-wind
býst	prepares
býstu	prepared

D, d

Old Icelandic	English
dag	day
daginn	the-day
dagur	day
danaher	Danish-forces
danakonungur	king-of-Denmark
Danmerkur	Denmark (place)
djörfung	bold
dögum	days
dóm	deeming
drakk	drank
drekk	drink
drekka	drank, drink, to-drink
drekki	drink
drekkur	drank
drengskap	honour
drengur	fellow
drjúgum	greatly
drottning	the-queen
drukkið	drunk
drukku	drinking
drykki	drank, drink
drykkju	drinking, drinks
dveljast	stay
dýrshorn	stag-horn

E, e

Old Icelandic	English
eða	but, or
ef	if
efna	carry-out
eftir	after, behind, remained, remaining
eg	I, I-am
eiga	own
eigi	none, not, one
eignast	own
einhverja	one-such
einkum	especially
einn	one
einnhvern	one-such
eins	alone
einsætt	clearly
einskis	no, nothing
eitt	one
ekki	not
eldist	old-is
ellegar	otherwise
elli	old-age

Word List (Old Icelandic to English)

Old Icelandic	English
eltast	chased
em	am
en	and, as, But, than, that, then, while, who
enda	and, conclude, end
enga	no
engan	no, only
engi	none
engis	nothing
Englandsfari	England-Traveller (name)
engu	none
enn	but, still, then, was
er	am, as, had, have, is, it-is, that, was, were, what, when, where, which, who
erindlaust	errand-without
ert	are
ertu	are-you
eru	are, there-are, they, they-were, were

F, f

Old Icelandic	English
fá	gave, get, give, pay
faðir	father
fæ	give
fæð	sadness
fær	accomplished, brought, travel
færa	brought
færi	bring, travel, went
færið	bring
færir	brought
fært	bringing
fagnaðartíðindi	good-news
fái	get
fáið	give
fáir	few
falar	bargain
falslaust	without-fraud
fám	a-few
fámæltur	of-few-words
fann	found

Old Icelandic	English
fara	go, going, travel, travelling, went
fararefni	travel-goods
fari	travel
farið	travel, travelled
farir	travel
fars	travel
fastara	more-fixedly
fátt	few
fé	payment
fegnir	celebrated
féið	wealth
fengi	found
fengið	got
fénu	wealth
fer	goes, went
ferðir	travel
festa	fasten
finnumst	found
fjárheimta	money-insisting
fjöldi	many
fleiri	more
floti	floating
flytja	carried
föður	father
fór	did, travelled, went
för	going
fórstu	went-you
förunauta	companions
förunautar	companions
föruneyti	companionship
fótum	feed
frá	from
fram	forward, forwards, from
framarla	forward
framgjarn	ambitious
fríður	handsome
fullreynt	fully-tested
fund	find, meet, to-meet
fundust	met
fylgdi	follow
fylgdina	following
fylgir	following
fylgja	follow
fyndust	found

Word List (Old Icelandic to English)

Old Icelandic	English
fyrir	along, before, for
fyrr	before
fyrra	the-first
fyrsta	first
fyrstu	first
fýsir	desire

G, g

Old Icelandic	English
gæði	good-things
gærkveld	last-night
gæta	take-care
gaf	gave
gáfu	gave
gáfuð	gave
gálga	gallows
galst	payment
gamall	old
gamalmenni	old-men
ganga	go
Garðaríki	Gardariki (place)
gefa	give, to-give
gefinn	given
gegnum	through
gekk	went
gelst	paid
gengu	went
gengur	going, went
gera	did, do, get, to-do
gerði	did
gerir	went
gerist	be
gersemar	treasure, treasures
gersemum	treasure
gert	done
get	get
gjalda	pay
gjaldið	payment, the-payment
gjöfin	gift
gjöfina	the-gift
gjörla	completely
glaðari	gladness
glymur	echo
góð	good
goða	the-priest
góður	good
greiða	assist
gulls	gold
gyldist	repay

H, h

Old Icelandic	English
hægt	possible
hærra	higher, highest
hæsta	highest
hættir	way
haf	sea
hafa	had, have, having, to-have, to-sea
hafði	had
hafi	had, has
hafið	have
hafir	have
hafs	sea
haft	had
halda	held, to-hold
haldast	hold
hálf	half
Halldór	Halldor (name)
Halldóri	Halldor (name)
Halldórs	Halldor (name), Halldor's (name)
hálm	straw, the-straw
halt	hold
haltu	hold-you
hann	he, him, it
hans	him, his
Harald	Harald (name)
Haraldi	Harald (name)
Haralds	Harald (name)
Haraldsslátta	Harald's-money (name)
Haraldur	Harald (name)
háseta	crew, sailors
hásetar	sailors
hásetum	sailors
háski	dangers
hausti	the-autumn
héðan	from-here, hence

Word List (Old Icelandic to English)

Old Icelandic	English
hefði	had
hefi	have
hefir	had, has, has-been, have, we-have
heilastan	thanks
heimfúsari	home-longing
heimta	drew
heimtir	got
heldur	hold, rather
helmings	half
helst	rather
helsti	rather
hendi	hand
hér	forces, here
herra	lord
hét	named, promised, was-named
heyra	hear
heyrðuð	heard
heyrum	hear
hin	the
hinn	the
hirðar	court
hirðina	guardsmen
hirðinni	court
hirðmaður	court-man
hirðsiðum	king's-men-customs
hitt	find
hitta	find
hitti	found
hittir	found
Hjarðarholti	Hjardarholt (place)
hlaupa	to-run
hleypur	run
hljóp	ran
hlut	part, share
hluti	part, things
hlutum	things
hlutur	part
hlýða	listen-to
hlýs	warmth
höfðu	had
hófi	modest
höndum	hand
honum	as-him, he, him, to-him
horn	horn
hornblástur	horn-blast
hornið	the-drinking-horn
hornsins	the-horn
hríð	awhile
hring	a-ring
hringinga	bell-ringing
hringingum	bell-ringing
hringinn	the-ring
hringja	ring
húðfat	hammock
hug	think
hún	she
hurfu	disappeared
hús	house
hvað	what
hvegi	which
hver	each, where, who
hverju	each
hverjum	who
hvern	which
hvers	how, what
hversu	how-so
hvert	each
hví	why
hvor	each
hvorki	neither
hvort	each, how, which
hygg	think

I, i

Old Icelandic	English
illa	badly, ill
inn	inside

Í, í

Old Icelandic	English
í	about, at, from, in, into, of, out-of, that, to, will, with
ígangsklæði	travelling-clothes
Ísland	Iceland (place)
Íslandi	Icelander (name)
Íslands	Iceland (place)

Word List (Old Icelandic to English)

Old Icelandic	English
íslenskan	Icelander

J, j

Old Icelandic	English
jafnfylginn	equally-following
jafnmjög	equally-much
jafntraustan	equally-trustworthy
jafntraustir	equally-trustworthy
jóla	Yule (name)
jólanna	Yule (name)
jólin	Yule (name)
Jólum	Yule (name)

K, k

Old Icelandic	English
kæmi	come
kærleikum	dearly-loved
kaf	overboard
kalla	called
kallað	called
kann	can, know
kappgjarn	self-willed
kaupa	purchase
Kaupangi	Kaupang (place)
kaupferðir	trading-voyages
kaupir	bought
kaupmaður	trading-man
kaupmenn	merchants, the-merchants, the-traders
kaupsveinar	trading-men
kemur	came
kennduð	taught
kertisveinar	court-men
kjósa	choose
klokkurum	clocks
knörr	ship
kom	came
koma	came, come, coming
komið	come
kominn	come, coming
komir	come
komu	came
konung	the-king
konunga	the-king
konungi	king, the-king, to-the-king
konungs	the-king, the-king's
konungsmenn	the-kings-men
konungsskipinu	the-king's-ship
konungsstofunni	the-king's-chambers
konungur	king, the-king
kopars	copper
kostar	choice
kosti	benefit
krefja	demand
kunnigt	known
kvað	said
kvaddi	called
kvaðst	said
kveld	evening
kyrrt	peace

L, l

Old Icelandic	English
lá	lay
lætur	behave, leave, let
lagi	had
land	land, the-land
landa	lands
landi	land, lands, the-land
lands	land
landtjald	land-tents
langskip	longships
lát	let-it
láta	allow, have, losing
láti	have
launuð	repaid
leggi	lay
leggja	grant
leggjum	lay
leggur	laid
leið	pass, passed, way
leita	seek
leitað	consider
lendir	landed
lendra	is-paid, payment
lendur	land
lengi	long

Word List (Old Icelandic to English)

Old Icelandic	English
lengur	longer
lést	had
lét	had
léti	let
léttlætiskonum	prostitutes
leyfa	allow
leyfi	leave
liði	crew, men
liðið	passed
líður	passed
lifa	life
líka	like
líkaði	liked
líst	appears
líta	look
lítill	little
litlu	little
lítt	little
lítur	looked
loftinu	the-air
lögðu	laid
logist	cheated
lokið	ended
lönd	land
löng	long
lygi	lie
lyndi	temper
Lyrgju	Lyrgja (place)
lýstur	struck

M, m

Old Icelandic	English
má	may
maður	a-man, man
mæðist	tired
mælt	spoken, spoken-of
mælti	spoke, spoke-to
mæltuð	spoke
mætti	may, might, might
mál	conversed, matter, measure
mála	matter, payment, payment
málagjöfina	payment
málann	payment
málanum	payment
málasilfrið	silverware
máli	matter, payment, speak
málið	matter
mann	man
manna	men, people, people's
mannháska	human-danger
marga	many
margur	many
matar	food
máttu	may, may-you
með	along, between, with
mega	may
megi	may
meir	more
meira	more
meiri	greater, more
melrakkabelgi	arctic-fox-furs
menn	men, people
mér	me, to-me, with-me
mesta	most
mesti	most
mig	me
mikið	huge
mikill	a-great, great
mikinn	greatly, much
mikla	much
Miklagarði	The-Great-City (place)
miklu	a-great, much
miklum	much
milli	between
mín	me, mine
mína	mine
minn	mine
minna	less
minni	mine
mínu	my
mislíkaði	misliked
mitt	mine, my
mjög	much
mönnum	people
morgun	morning, the-morning
mörk	a-mark
mót	return

Word List (Old Icelandic to English)

Old Icelandic	English
móti	meet, meeting
mótinu	the-meeting
móts	meet
mótsins	the-meeting
möttulsskauti	cloak-lap
mun	could, shall, should, would
mundi	should, would
mundir	would
mundu	should, would
muni	shall
munkat	shall
munt	must
muntu	should
munum	shall, should
myrgininn	morning

N, n

Old Icelandic	English
næst	next
næsta	next, next-to
næstum	before
nætur	night
nakkvað	something
nálega	nearly
nauðgað	force
nauðsyn	necessity
né	nor
neðan	below
neitt	nothing
nema	except, take
neyta	use
neytti	consumed
Nið	Nid (place)
níðist	down
niður	below, down
nóga	enough
nokkuð	something, somewhat
nokkur	something
nokkura	some
nokkurum	some
norður	north
Noreg	Norway (place)
Noregi	Norway (place)
Noregs	Norway (place)
norrænir	Norwegians
nótt	night
nú	now

O, o

Old Icelandic	English
of	over
oft	often
oftar	frequent, more-often
og	also, and
okkar	ours
okkur	our, us
orð	word, words, word-to
orðaframkast	outburst
orði	word
orðsending	word-sending
oss	to-us, us

Ó, ó

Old Icelandic	English
ófriðar	hostilities
ófriðinn	un-peace
ófriður	un-peace
ófús	unwilling
óglaðari	un-gladness
ógladdist	un-glad
ómaklega	undeservedly
ómjúkur	un-bending
ónýttir	un-used
Ósló	Oslo (place)
ósýnt	unseen
ótiginn	un-high-born
óvingjarnlega	unfriendly

Ö, ö

Old Icelandic	English
öðru	a-second
öðrum	other
öllu	all
öllum	all

Word List (Old Icelandic to English)

Old Icelandic	English
P, p	
prettunum	trick
R, r	
ráð	advise, the-matter
ráða	prevail
ráðagerðir	advice-giving
ráðast	appoint, arrange
ráðið	hired
ráðist	decide
ræðst	commanded
ræður	leading
reiði	anger
reiðist	commanded
rekið	thrown
rekkju	bed
reyki	smoke
reyna	know
ríki	kingdom
ró	rest
rúmi	seat
rúms	room
S, s	
sá	so
sæmd	honour
sæmilegt	the-same
sættast	reconcile
sagði	said
sagt	is-said, said
sakar	the-sake-of
saman	together
samir	so
sat	sat, stayed
satt	be-true, true
sátu	sat
sáu	saw
sé	is, see, so
seg	say
segir	said, told
segja	say, told
segl	the-sails
seilast	to-reach
sein	late
seint	late, slow, slowly
sel	flip
sem	as, that, was, which
semja	negotiate
senda	send
sendi	sent
sér	for, he, him, himself, saw, themselves
sérð	see
sért	be
sessunautar	sitting-together
setja	sit
setjið	set
settust	sat
sex	six
síð	later
síðan	afterwards, since, then
síðar	afterwards, later
síðast	the-last
síðkveldum	late-evening
síður	less
sig	him
sigldu	sailed
siglingum	sailing
Sigurður	Sigurd (name)
silfrið	the-silver
silfrinu	the-silver
silfur	silver
sín	him, theirs
sína	his
sínar	theirs
sinn	he, his
sinni	his, themselves, time, yourself
síns	his
sínu	his, their
sínum	his
síst	least
sitja	settle
sitt	his
situr	sat

80

Word List (Old Icelandic to English)

Old Icelandic	English
sjá	see, so
sjálfir	themselves
sjáum	we-see
skaða	damages
skal	shall
skálum	bowl
skammt	short-distance
skap	mood
skapi	mood
skapkers	large-vessel
skaplyndi	mood-temper
skark	noise
skerið	a-rock
skildust	separated
skilja	separate
skilnaður	parting
skilur	separated
skip	a-ship, ship, ships, the-ship
skipagangur	shipping
skipan	ships
skipi	a-ship, ship
skipið	ship, the-ship
skipinu	ship, the-ship
skips	a-ship, ships
skipsins	ship
skipstjórn	ship-steering
skipstjórnar	ship-steer
skipum	ships
skipun	crew
skipverðsins	ship's-worth
skipverja	the-crew
skíran	cleared
skírt	pure
skjótt	swift, swiftly
skorti	shortly
skotið	launched
skuli	shall
skulu	should
skuluð	should
skulum	shall
skyggt	shaded
skyldi	should
skyldu	should
skyti	shot
skýtur	launched
sleit	broken-up
sleitilega	unfairly
slíkra	such
slíkri	such
slíkt	such
slíku	such
slóst	struck
snemma	early, soon
Snorra	Snorri (name)
Snorrason	Snorrason (name)
Snorrasyni	Snorrason (name)
snúa	turned
sofa	sleep
sögð	told
sögðu	said
sóma	honour
sömu	the-same
spilli	spoil
spurði	asked
spyr	asked
stað	replace
stafninn	the-prow
stefnið	heading
stendur	stands, stood
stirðlæti	hard-temper
stjórnar	steer
stóð	stood
stóðu	stood
stórættaður	of-high-family
stórmennsku	greatness
strangt	strange
stríðu	stressful
stuttorður	short-worded
stygglyndur	quick-tempered
stýrði	steered
stýrimaður	steersman
stýrimanns	the-steersman
styrkastur	strongest
stytti	short
suður	south
sumarið	summer
sumir	some
sumrum	summers
sundur	separate
svaf	slept

Word List (Old Icelandic to English)

Old Icelandic	English
sváfu	slept
svarar	answered
sveinar	fellows
Sveini	Svein (name)
sveinn	fellow, Svein (name), the-fellow
svívirðing	disgrace
svívirðlega	dishonourable
svívirður	dishonourable
svo	so
sýndist	seemed
synir	sons
sýnist	seemed
sýnum	in-appearance
sýr	Sow

T, t

Old Icelandic	English
taka	take
tala	speak
tek	take
tekið	taken
tekur	took
tíðast	swiftly
tíðindi	tidings
til	about, for, to, until
tíska	custom
títt	immediately
tók	took
tóku	took
tólf	twelve
trúa	believe

Þ, þ

Old Icelandic	English
þá	them, then
það	it, that, this
þætti	seems
þakkaði	thanked
þakkar	thanked
þangað	from-there
þann	it, then
þannug	that-way
þar	there, there, they
þarf	needed
þatgi	that-not
þau	them, then
þegar	straightaway, straightaway, there
þeim	of-them, them, they
þeir	the, there, they
þekkjast	accept
þenna	that
þér	to-you, you, you-to
þess	is-this, like-this, that, these, this, those
þessi	these, this
þessu	this
þessum	those
þetta	it, that, this
þig	you
þín	your
þína	yours
þínar	you
þinn	your, yours
þínum	yours
þitt	yours
þjóna	serve
þjónað	served
þjónusta	service
þjónustu	service
þjónustumenn	servants
þó	though
þokkar	favours
þörf	needed
Þóri	Thorir (name)
Þórir	Thorir (name), Thorir (name)
Þóris	Thorir's (name)
þótt	though
þóttist	thought
Þrándheimi	Trondheim (place)
Þrándheims	Trondheim (place)
þrenna	treble
þrjú	three
þú	you
þurfa	needed, you-need
því	accordingly, because, of, that, therefore, with

Word List (Old Icelandic to English)

Old Icelandic	English
þyki	think
þykir	seemed, thinks, thought
þykist	think
þykja	think
þykjast	consider

U, u

Old Icelandic	English
um	about
umræða	discussion
undan	away-from, from-under, under
undir	under
undirhluturinn	the-under-part
unnið	deserved
upp	up, upped
uppi	up
upplenskur	an-Upplander
upplost	false-rumour
urðu	became
utan	out

Ú, ú

Old Icelandic	English
úr	from, out-of
úrræða	solution
út	out, out-of
útferð	out-travelling
úti	outside

V, v

Old Icelandic	English
vægð	grace
vændiskonum	prostitutes
vænna	expected
væri	had, was
vakna	awoke
vaknar	awoke
vald	power
vandi	custom
vandskipaður	difficult
vant	difficult, expected
var	was, were
varð	became, was
varðveita	guard-over
varla	hardly
vega	weigh
vegur	way
veislum	the-feasts
veislur	feasts
veist	know
veistu	know-you
veit	know
veita	grant, lead
vel	well
velja	will
ver	be
vér	we
vera	be, becoming, being, is, it-be
verð	worth
verða	be, to-be
verðum	worth
verður	came, worth
verið	be, been, being, had-been
verja	spend
verr	worse
verri	worse
verst	becomes
vert	worth, worthy
vetur	winter
veturinn	winter
vexti	well-built
við	against, with
víghug	killing-mind
Vík	Vik (place)
vil	will, wish
vildi	willed, wish, wished
vilgis	very
vilja	wish
vilji	willed
viljum	wish, wish-to
vill	willed, wished, wished-to, wishes
vilt	wish
vinar	friend
vináttu	friendship

Word List (Old Icelandic to English)

Old Icelandic	English
vinda	wind
vingan	friendship
vingjarnleg	friendly
vinna	to-win-over
vinur	friend
vinveitt	favourable
virðing	honour, worthiness
viskur	wise
víst	certainly
vistum	provisions
vísu	certainly
vita	certainly, know
víti	punishment, signalled
vitið	know
vítið	penalty, the-penalty
vítin	penalty
vítishornið	penalty-horn
vitni	testimony
víttur	penalty, reprimanded
vopndjarfastur	weapons-bold
vopnum	weapons
vor	our
vora	going, spring
vorið	spring
vort	ours
voru	were
votir	wet
voveiflega	unexpected

Y, y

Old Icelandic	English
yðrar	yours
yður	you
yðvars	yours
yfir	over
yfirbragði	complexion
ykkar	with-you
ykkra	yours
ykkur	you-two
yrði	became

Ý, ý

Old Icelandic	English
ýkva	veer
ýmissa	various

Word List *(English to Old Icelandic)*

English	Old Icelandic

A, a

English	Old Icelandic
a-ban	bann
about	á, í, til, um
accept	þekkjast
access	atgang
accomplished	fær
accordingly	því
advice-giving	ráðagerðir
advise	ráð
a-few	fám
after	aftur, eftir
afterwards	síðan, síðar
against	við
age	ævi
a-great	mikill, miklu
all	allir, allir, allra, allt, allt, öllu, öllum
all-long	alllangt
allow	láta, leyfa
all-prepared	albúnir
alone	eins
along	fyrir, með
also	og
am	em, er
a-man	maður
a-mark	mörk
ambitious	framgjarn
ancestry	ætt
and	á, en, enda, og
anger	reiði
another	annan, annan, annars, annars
answered	svarar
an-Upplander	upplenskur
appears	líst
appoint	ráðast
arctic-fox-furs	melrakkabelgi
are	ert, eru
are-you	ertu
a-ring	hring
a-rock	skerið
arrange	ráðast
as	á, en, er, sem
a-second	öðru
as-him	honum
a-ship	skip, skipi, skips
asked	beiða, beitt, biður, spurði, spyr
assist	greiða
at	á, að, í
a-trick	brögð
away	brott
away-from	undan
away-prepared	brautbúnaði
awhile	hríð
awoke	vakna, vaknar

B, b

English	Old Icelandic
back	aftur
badly	illa
ban	bannar
Bard (name)	Bárður
bargain	falar
be	gerist, sért, ver, vera, verða, verið
bear	bera, beri
bears	ber
became	urðu, varð, yrði
because	því
becomes	verst
becoming	vera
bed	rekkju
been	verið
before	áður, fyrir, fyrr, næstum
began	byrjaði
behave	lætur
behind	eftir
being	vera, verið
believe	trúa
bell-ringing	hringinga, hringingum
below	neðan, niður

Word List (English to Old Icelandic)

English	*Old Icelandic*	English	*Old Icelandic*
benefit	*kosti*	companionship	*föruneyti*
best	*bergst, best, besta*	completely	*gjörla*
be-true	*satt*	complexion	*yfirbragði*
better	*betra, betur*	conclude	*enda*
between	*með, milli*	consider	*leitað, þykjast*
bid	*báðu, biður*	consumed	*neytti*
bold	*djörfung*	conversed	*mál*
bore	*bar*	copper	*kopars*
both	*báðum, bæði*	could	*mun*
bought	*kaupir*	court	*hirðar, hirðinni*
bowl	*skálum*	court-man	*hirðmaður*
Bratteyar (place)	*Bröttueyri*	court-men	*kertisveinar*
breaking	*brjótist*	crew	*áhöfnina, háseta, liði, skipun*
bring	*færi, færið*		
bringing	*bar, fært*	custom	*tíska, vandi*
broken-up	*sleit*		
brought	*fær, færa, færir*		
burnt	*brennda*		
but	*eða, en, enn*		

C, c

D, d

English	*Old Icelandic*
called	*kalla, kallað, kvaddi*
calling	*ákallsi*
came	*kemur, kom, koma, komu, verður*
can	*kann*
carried	*ber, flytja*
carry-out	*efna*
celebrated	*fegnir*
certainly	*víst, vísu, vita*
changed	*breytt*
chased	*eltast*
cheated	*logist*
choice	*kostar*
choose	*kjósa*
cleared	*skíran*
clearly	*einsætt*
cloak-lap	*möttulsskauti*
clocks	*klokkurum*
come	*kæmi, koma, komið, kominn, komir*
coming	*koma, kominn*
commanded	*ræðst, reiðist*
companions	*förunauta, förunautar*

English	*Old Icelandic*
damages	*skaða*
dangers	*háski*
Danish-forces	*danaher*
day	*dag, dagur*
days	*dögum*
dearly-loved	*kærleikum*
decide	*ráðist*
deeming	*dóm*
demand	*krefja*
Denmark (place)	*Danmerkur*
deserved	*unnið*
desire	*fýsir*
did	*fór, gera, gerði*
difficult	*vandskipaður, vant*
direction	*beint*
disappeared	*hurfu*
discussion	*umræða*
disgrace	*svívirðing*
dishonourable	*svívirðlega, svívirður*
do	*gera*
done	*gert*
down	*níðist, niður*
drank	*drakk, drekka, drekkur, drykki*
drew	*heimta*
drink	*drekk, drekka, drekki, drykki*

Word List (English to Old Icelandic)

English	Old Icelandic
drinking	*drukku, drykkju*
drinks	*drykkju*
drunk	*drukkið*

E, e

English	Old Icelandic
each	*hver, hverju, hvert, hvor, hvort*
early	*snemma*
early-riser	*árrisull*
east	*austan, austur, austur*
echo	*glymur*
eighth	*átti*
end	*enda*
ended	*lokið*
England-Traveller (name)	*Englandsfari*
enough	*nóga*
equally-following	*jafnfylginn*
equally-much	*jafnmjög*
equally-trustworthy	*jafntraustan, jafntraustir*
errand-without	*erindlaust*
especially	*einkum*
evening	*aftan, aftna, kveld*
except	*nema*
expected	*vænna, vant*

F, f

English	Old Icelandic
fair-wind	*byr*
false-rumour	*upplost*
farmed	*bjó*
fasten	*festa*
father	*faðir, föður*
favourable	*vinveitt*
favours	*þokkar*
feasts	*veislur*
feed	*fótum*
fellow	*drengur, sveinn*
fellows	*sveinar*
few	*fáir, fátt*
find	*fund, hitt, hitta*
first	*fyrsta, fyrstu*

English	Old Icelandic
flip	*sel*
floating	*floti*
follow	*fylgdi, fylgja*
following	*fylgdina, fylgir*
food	*matar*
for	*fyrir, sér, til*
force	*nauðgað*
forces	*hér*
foreclose	*bregða*
forward	*fram, framarla*
forwards	*fram*
found	*fann, fengi, finnumst, fyndust, hitti, hittir*
frequent	*oftar*
friend	*vinar, vinur*
friendly	*vingjarnleg*
friendship	*vináttu, vingan*
from	*af, af, frá, fram, í, úr*
from-here	*héðan*
from-there	*þangað*
from-under	*undan*
fully-tested	*fullreynt*
furs	*belgi*

G, g

English	Old Icelandic
gallows	*gálga*
Gardariki (place)	*Garðaríki*
gave	*bar, fá, gaf, gáfu, gáfuð*
get	*fá, fái, gera, get*
gift	*gjöfin*
give	*fá, fæ, fáið, gefa*
given	*gefinn*
gladness	*glaðari*
go	*fara, ganga*
goes	*fer*
going	*fara, för, gengur, vora*
gold	*gulls*
good	*góð, góður*
good-news	*fagnaðartíðindi*
good-things	*gæði*
got	*fengið, heimtir*
grace	*vægð*
grant	*leggja, veita*

Word List (English to Old Icelandic)

English	Old Icelandic	English	Old Icelandic
great	*mikill*	himself	*sér*
greater	*meiri*	hired	*ráðið*
greatly	*drjúgum, mikinn*	his	*hans, sína, sinn, sinni, síns, sínu, sínum, sitt*
greatness	*stórmennsku*		
guard-over	*varðveita*		
guardsmen	*hirðina*	Hjardarholt (place)	*Hjarðarholti*
		hold	*haldast, halt, heldur*

H, h

		hold-you	*haltu*
		home-longing	*heimfúsari*
had	*á, átti, er, hafa, hafði, hafi, haft, hefði, hefir, höfðu, lagi, lést, lét, væri*	honour	*drengskap, sæmd, sóma, virðing*
		horn	*horn*
		horn-blast	*hornblástur*
		hostilities	*ófriðar*
had-been	*verið*	house	*hús*
half	*hálf, helmings*	how	*hvers, hvort*
Halldor (name)	*Halldór, Halldóri, Halldórs*	how-so	*hversu*
		huge	*mikið*
Halldor's (name)	*Halldórs*	human-danger	*mannháska*
hammock	*húðfat*		
hand	*hendi, höndum*		
handsome	*fríður*		

I, i

happiest	*blíðast*		
happily	*blíðlegur*	I	*eg*
Harald (name)	*Harald, Haraldi, Haralds, Haraldur*	I-am	*eg*
		Iceland (place)	*Ísland, Íslands*
Harald's-money (name)	*Haraldsslátta*	Icelander	*íslenskan*
		Icelander (name)	*Íslandi*
hardly	*varla*	if	*ef*
hard-temper	*stirðlæti*	ill	*illa*
has	*hafi, hefir*	immediately	*títt*
has-been	*hefir*	in	*á, að, í*
have	*er, hafa, hafið, hafir, hefi, hefir, láta, láti*	in-appearance	*sýnum*
		in-on	*að*
having	*hafa*	inside	*inn*
he	*hann, honum, sér, sinn*	intend	*ætla*
		intended	*ætlað, ætlaði, ætlar, ætlist*
heading	*stefnið*		
hear	*heyra, heyrum*	intends	*ætlar*
heard	*heyrðuð*	into	*í*
held	*halda*	invitation	*boð*
hence	*héðan*	is	*á, er, sé, vera*
here	*hér*	is-paid	*lendra*
higher	*hærra*	is-said	*sagt*
highest	*hærra, hæsta*	is-this	*þess*
him	*hann, hans, honum, sér, sig, sín*		

Word List (English to Old Icelandic)

English	Old Icelandic
it	*að, hann, það, þann, þetta*
it-be	*vera*
it-is	*er*

J, j

joyful	*blíðu*

K, k

Kaupang (place)	*Kaupangi*
keep-asking	*brekar*
killing-mind	*víghug*
king	*konungi, konungur*
kingdom	*ríki*
king-of-Denmark	*danakonungur*
king's-men-customs	*hirðsiðum*
know	*kann, reyna, veist, veit, vita, vitið*
known	*kunnigt*
know-you	*veistu*

L, l

laid	*leggur, lögðu*
land	*land, landi, lands, lendur, lönd*
landed	*lendir*
lands	*landa, landi*
land-tents	*landtjald*
large-vessel	*skapkers*
last-night	*gærkveld*
late	*sein, seint*
late-evening	*síðkveldum*
later	*síð, síðar*
launched	*skotið, skýtur*
lay	*lá, leggi, leggjum*
lead	*veita*
leading	*ræður*
least	*síst*
leave	*lætur, leyfi*
less	*minna, síður*
let	*lætur, léti*

English	Old Icelandic
let-it	*lát*
lie	*lygi*
life	*lifa*
like	*líka*
liked	*líkaði*
like-this	*þess*
listen-to	*hlýða*
little	*lítill, litlu, lítt*
long	*lengi, löng*
longer	*lengur*
longships	*langskip*
look	*líta*
looked	*lítur*
lord	*herra*
losing	*láta*
Lyrgja (place)	*Lyrgju*

M, m

man	*maður, mann*
many	*fjöldi, marga, margur*
matter	*mál, mála, máli, málið*
may	*má, mætti, máttu, mega, megi*
may-you	*máttu*
me	*mér, mig, mín*
measure	*mál*
meet	*fund, móti, móts*
meeting	*móti*
men	*liði, manna, menn*
merchants	*kaupmenn*
merchant-ship	*byrðing*
met	*fundust*
might	*mætti, mætti*
mine	*mín, mína, minn, minni, mitt*
misliked	*mislíkaði*
modest	*hófi*
moment	*bili*
money-insisting	*fjárheimta*
mood	*skap, skapi*
mood-temper	*skaplyndi*
more	*fleiri, meir, meira, meiri*
more-fixedly	*fastara*

Word List (English to Old Icelandic)

English	Old Icelandic
more-often	oftar
morning	morgun, myrgininn
most	mesta, mesti
much	mikinn, mikla, miklu, miklum, mjög
must	munt
my	mínu, mitt

N, n

English	Old Icelandic
named	hét
nearly	nálega
necessity	nauðsyn
needed	þarf, þörf, þurfa
negotiate	semja
neither	hvorki
next	næst, næsta
next-to	næsta
Nid (place)	Nið
night	nætur, nótt
no	einskis, enga, engan
noise	skark
none	eigi, engi, engu
nor	né
north	norður
Norway (place)	Noreg, Noregi, Noregs
Norwegians	norrænir
not	eigi, ekki
nothing	einskis, engis, neitt
now	nú

O, o

English	Old Icelandic
of	á, að, af, af, í, því
of-all	allra
of-few-words	fámæltur
of-high-family	stórættaður
often	oft
of-them	þeim
old	gamall
old-age	elli
old-is	eldist
old-men	gamalmenni
on	á
one	eigi, einn, eitt
one-such	einhverja, einnhvern
only	engan
on-the	á
or	eða
Oslo (place)	Ósló
other	aðra, aðrir, áður, annarra, annarri, öðrum
otherwise	ellegar
ounces	aura
our	okkur, vor
ours	okkar, vort
out	út, utan
outburst	orðaframkast
out-of	í, úr, út
outside	úti
outspoken	bermæltur
out-travelling	útferð
over	of, yfir
overboard	kaf
own	eiga, eignast

P, p

English	Old Icelandic
paid	gelst
part	hlut, hluti, hlutur
parting	skilnaður
pass	leið
passed	leið, liðið, líður
pay	fá, gjalda
payment	fé, galst, gjaldið, lendra, mála, mála, málagjöfina, málann, málanum, máli
peace	kyrrt
penalty	vítið, vítin, víttur
penalty-horn	vítishornið
people	manna, menn, mönnum
people's	manna
possible	hægt
power	vald
preparations	bjuggu, búnaðinn

Word List (English to Old Icelandic)

English	*Old Icelandic*	English	*Old Icelandic*
prepared	*búa, búið, búinn, býr, býstu*	sailing	*siglingum*
prepares	*býst*	sailors	*háseta, hásetar, hásetum*
prevail	*ráða*	sat	*sat, sátu, settust, situr*
promised	*hét*	saw	*sáu, sér*
promising-wind	*byrvænlegt*	say	*seg, segja*
prostitutes	*léttlætiskonum, vændiskonum*	sea	*haf, hafs*
provisions	*vistum*	seat	*rúmi*
punishment	*víti*	see	*sé, sérð, sjá*
purchase	*kaupa*	seek	*leita*
pure	*skírt*	seemed	*sýndist, sýnist, þykir*
		seems	*þætti*

Q, q

quick-tempered	*stygglyndur*

R, r

English	*Old Icelandic*
ran	*hljóp*
rather	*heldur, helst, helsti*
reacted	*brygði*
readied	*bjóst*
reconcile	*sættast*
remained	*eftir*
remaining	*eftir*
repaid	*launuð*
repaired	*bætt*
repay	*gyldist*
replace	*stað*
reprimanded	*víttur*
resolved	*alugað*
rest	*ró*
return	*mót*
ring	*hringja*
room	*rúms*
run	*hleypur*

English	*Old Icelandic*
self-willed	*kappgjarn*
send	*senda*
sent	*sendi*
separate	*skilja, sundur*
separated	*skildust, skilur*
servants	*þjónustumenn*
serve	*þjóna*
served	*þjónað*
service	*þjónusta, þjónustu*
set	*setjið*
settle	*bú, byggja, sitja*
settled	*bjó*
shaded	*skyggt*
shall	*mun, muni, munkat, munum, skal, skuli, skulum*
share	*hlut*
she	*hún*
ship	*knörr, skip, skipi, skipið, skipinu, skipsins*
shipping	*skipagangur*
ships	*skip, skipan, skips, skipum*
ship-steer	*skipstjórnar*
ship-steering	*skipstjórn*
ship's-worth	*skipverðsins*
short	*stytti*
short-distance	*skammt*
shortly	*skorti*
short-worded	*stuttorður*
shot	*skyti*
should	*mun, mundi, mundu, muntu, munum, skulu, skuluð, skyldi, skyldu*

S, s

English	*Old Icelandic*
sadness	*fæð*
said	*kvað, kvaðst, sagði, sagt, segir, sögðu*
sailed	*sigldu*

Word List (English to Old Icelandic)

English	Old Icelandic	English	Old Icelandic
signalled	*víti*	strange	*strangt*
Sigurd (name)	*Sigurður*	straw	*hálm*
silver	*silfur*	stress	*álaga*
silverware	*málasilfrið*	stressful	*stríðu*
since	*síðan*	strongest	*styrkastur*
sit	*setja*	struck	*lýstur, slóst*
sitting-together	*sessunautar*	such	*slíkra, slíkri, slíkt, slíku*
six	*sex*		
sleep	*sofa*	summer	*sumarið*
slept	*svaf, sváfu*	summers	*sumrum*
slow	*seint*	suppose	*ætla*
slowly	*seint*	Svein (name)	*Sveini, Sveinn*
smoke	*reyki*	swift	*skjótt*
Snorrason (name)	*Snorrason, Snorrasyni*	swiftly	*skjótt, tíðast*

T, t

English	Old Icelandic
Snorri (name)	*Snorra*
so	*sá, samir, sé, sjá, svo*
solution	*úrræða*
some	*nokkura, nokkurum, sumir*
something	*nakkvað, nokkuð, nokkur*
somewhat	*nokkuð*
sons	*synir*
soon	*snemma*
south	*suður*
Sow	*sýr*
speak	*máli, tala*
spend	*verja*
spoil	*spilli*
spoke	*mælti, mæltuð*
spoken	*mælt*
spoken-of	*mælt*
spoke-to	*mælti*
spring	*vora, vorið*
stag-horn	*dýrshorn*
stands	*stendur*
stay	*dveljast*
stayed	*sat*
steer	*stjórnar*
steered	*stýrði*
steersman	*stýrimaður*
still	*enn*
stood	*stendur, stóð, stóðu*
straightaway	*þegar*
straight-away	*þegar*

English	Old Icelandic
take	*nema, taka, tek*
take-care	*gæta*
taken	*tekið*
taught	*kennduð*
temper	*lyndi*
testimony	*vitni*
than	*en*
thanked	*þakkaði, þakkar*
thanks	*heilastan*
that	*á, að, en, er, í, sem, það, þenna, þess, þetta, því*
that-not	*þatgi*
that-way	*þannug*
the	*á, að, hin, hinn, þeir*
the-air	*loftinu*
the-anchor	*akkeri*
the-autumn	*hausti*
the-city	*bænum*
the-cockerel	*árgalinn*
the-crew	*skipverja*
the-day	*daginn*
the-drinking-horn	*hornið*
the-feasts	*veislum*
the-fellow	*sveinn*
the-first	*fyrra*
the-gift	*gjöfina*

Word List (English to Old Icelandic)

English	Old Icelandic	English	Old Icelandic
The-Great-City (place)	Miklagarði	they-were	eru
the-horn	hornsins	things	hluti, hlutum
their	sínu	think	hug, hygg, þyki, þykist, þykja
theirs	sín, sínar	thinks	þykir
the-king	konung, konunga, konungi, konungs, konungur	this	á, að, það, þess, þessi, þessu, þetta
the-king's	konungs	this-town	bænum
the-king's-chambers	konungsstofunni	Thorir (name)	Þóri, Þórir, Þórir
the-kings-men	konungsmenn	Thorir's (name)	Þóris
the-king's-ship	konungsskipinu	those	þess, þessum
the-land	land, landi	though	þó, þótt
the-last	síðast	thought	þóttist, þykir
them	þá, þau, þeim	three	þrjú
the-matter	ráð	through	gegnum
the-meeting	mótinu, mótsins	thrown	rekið
the-merchants	kaupmenn	tidings	tíðindi
the-morning	morgun	tied-up	bindur
themselves	sér, sinni, sjálfir	time	sinni
then	á, en, enn, síðan, þá, þann, þau	tired	mæðist
the-next	annan	to	á, að, í, til
the-payment	gjaldið	to-be	verða
the-penalty	vítið	to-come	aðkoma
the-priest	goða	to-do	gera
the-prow	stafninn	to-drink	drekka
the-queen	drottning	together	saman
there	þar, þar, þegar, þeir	to-give	gefa
there-are	eru	to-have	hafa
therefore	því	to-him	honum
the-ring	hringinn	to-hold	halda
the-river	ánni	told	segir, segja, sögð
the-sails	segl	to-me	mér
the-sake-of	sakar	to-meet	fund
the-same	sæmilegt, sömu	took	tekur, tók, tóku
these	þess, þessi	to-reach	seilast
the-ship	skip, skipið, skipinu	to-run	hlaupa
the-silver	silfrið, silfrinu	to-sea	hafa
the-steersman	stýrimanns	to-the-king	konungi
the-straw	hálm	to-us	oss
the-tow-boat	báti	to-win-over	vinna
the-town	bænum	town	bæinn
the-traders	kaupmenn	townspeople	bæjarmenn
the-under-part	undirhluturinn	to-you	þér
they	eru, þar, þeim, þeir	trading-man	kaupmaður
		trading-men	kaupsveinar
		trading-voyages	kaupferðir

Word List (English to Old Icelandic)

English	Old Icelandic
travel	*fær, færi, fara, fari, farið, farir, fars, ferðir*
travel-goods	*fararefni*
travelled	*farið, fór*
travelling	*fara*
travelling-clothes	*ígangsklæði*
treasure	*gersemar, gersemum*
treasures	*gersemar*
treble	*þrenna*
trick	*prettunum*
Trondheim (place)	*Þrándheimi, Þrándheims*
true	
trumpet-blown	*blásið*
turbulence	*aga*
turned	*snúa*
twelve	*tólf*

U, u

English	Old Icelandic
un-bending	*ómjúkur*
under	*undan, undir*
undeservedly	*ómaklega*
unexpected	*voveiflega*
unfairly	*sleitilega*
unfriendly	*óvingjarnlega*
un-glad	*ógladdist*
un-gladness	*óglaðari*
un-high-born	*ótiginn*
un-peace	*ófriðinn, ófriður*
unseen	*ósýnt*
until	*til*
un-used	*ónýttir*
unwilling	*ófús*
up	*upp, uppi*
upped	*upp*
us	*okkur, oss*
use	*neyta*

V, v

English	Old Icelandic
various	*ýmissa*
veer	*ýkva*
very	*vilgis*
Vik (place)	*Vík*
violated	*brotin*

W, w

English	Old Icelandic
wait	*bíð, bíða, biðleika*
warmth	*hlýs*
warn	*ávíta*
was	*enn, er, sem, væri, var, varð*
was-named	*hét*
way	*hættir, leið, vegur*
we	*vér*
wealth	*féið, fénu*
weapons	*vopnum*
weapons-bold	*vopndjarfastur*
we-have	*hefir*
weigh	*vega*
well	*vel*
well-built	*vexti*
went	*færi, fara, fer, fór, gekk, gengu, gengur, gerir*
went-you	*fórstu*
were	*er, eru, var, voru*
we-see	*sjáum*
wet	*votir*
what	*er, hvað, hvers*
when	*er*
where	*er, hver*
which	*er, hvegi, hvern, hvort, sem*
while	*en*
who	*en, er, hver, hverjum*
why	*hví*
will	*í, velja, vil*
willed	*vildi, vilji, vill*
wind	*vinda*
winter	*vetur, veturinn*
wise	*viskur*
wish	*vil, vildi, vilja, viljum, vilt*
wished	*vildi, vill*
wished-to	*vill*
wishes	*vill*

Word List (English to Old Icelandic)

English	Old Icelandic
wish-to	*viljum*
with	*í, með, því, við*
with-me	*mér*
without-fraud	*falslaust*
with-you	*ykkar*
word	*orð, orði*
words	*orð*
word-sending	*orðsending*
word-to	*orð*
worried-face	*áhyggjusvip*
worse	*verr, verri*
worth	*verð, verðum, verður, vert*
worthiness	*virðing*
worthy	*vert*
would	*mun, mundi, mundir, mundu*

Y, y

you	*þér, þig, þínar, þú, yður*
you-need	*þurfa*
your	*þín, þinn*
yours	*þína, þinn, þínum, þitt, yðrar, yðvars, ykkra*
yourself	*sinni*
you-to	*þér*
you-two	*ykkur*
Yule (name)	*jóla, jólanna, jólin, Jólum*

A Word Comparison of Old Norse and Old Icelandic Words

Old Norse	Old Icelandic	English
áðr	áður	before
áðr	áður	other
ætlast	ætlist	intended
ætlat	ætlað	intended
aftr	aftur	after
aftr	aftur	back
ákalsi	ákallsi	calling
ákkeri	akkeri	the-anchor
alhugat	alugað	resolved
at	að	at
at	að	in
at	að	in-on
at	að	it
at	að	of
at	að	that
at	að	the
at	að	this
at	að	to
austr	austur	east
Bárðr	Bárður	Bard (name)
bermæltr	bermæltur	outspoken
berr	ber	bears
berr	ber	carried
betr	betur	better
bezt	best	best
bezta	besta	best
biðleika,	biðleika	wait
biðr	biður	asked
biðr	biður	bid
bindr	bindur	tied-up
blásit	blásið	trumpet-blown
blíðligr	blíðlegur	happily
búit	búið	prepared
byrr	byr	fair-wind
byrvænligt	byrvænlegt	promising-wind
dagr	dagur	day

Old Norse	Old Icelandic	English
danakonungr	danakonungur	king-of-Denmark
Danmerkr	Danmerkur	Denmark (place)
drekka	drekki	drink
drekkr	drekkur	drank
drengr	drengur	fellow
dróttning	drottning	the-queen
drukkit	drukkið	drunk
ek	eg	I
ek	eg	I-am
elligar	ellegar	otherwise
enskis	einskis	no
erendlaust	erindlaust	errand-without
fá	fái	get
færr	fær	accomplished
færr	fær	travel
fagnaðartíðendi	fagnaðartíðindi	good-news
fái	fáið	give
fámæltr	fámæltur	of-few-words
fararefnin	fararefni	travel-goods
farit	farið	travel
farit	farið	travelled
fengit	fengið	got
ferr	fer	goes
ferr	fer	went
fét	féið	wealth
finnimst	finnumst	found
fjöldi	fjöldi	many
fórtu	fórstu	went-you
frændum	föður	father
fríðr	fríður	handsome
fylgði	fylgdi	follow
fylgðina	fylgdina	following
fyndist	fyndust	found
galzt	galst	payment
gelzt	gelst	paid
gengr	gengur	going

A Word Comparison of Old Norse and Old Icelandic

Old Norse	Old Icelandic	English
gengr	gengur	went
gerla	gjörla	completely
gersimar	gersemar	treasure
gersimar	gersemar	treasures
gersimum	gersemum	treasure
gjaldit	gjaldið	payment
gjaldit	gjaldið	the-payment
glymr	glymur	echo
góðr	góður	good
hæra	hærra	higher
hæra	hærra	highest
Halldórr	Halldór	Halldor (name)
Haraldr	Haraldur	Harald (name)
heðan	héðan	from-here
heðan	héðan	hence
heilstan	heilastan	thanks
heldr	heldur	hold
heldr	heldur	rather
helzt	helst	rather
helzti	helsti	rather
her	hér	here
hirðmaðr	hirðmaður	court-man
hleypr	hleypur	run
hlutr	hlutur	part
hon	hún	she
hornblástr	hornblástur	horn-blast
hornit	hornið	the-drinking-horn
hringingar	hringinga	bell-ringing
hvárki	hvorki	neither
hvárr	hvor	each
hvárt	hvort	each
hvárt	hvort	how
hvárt	hvort	which
hvat	hvað	what
hvégi	hvegi	which
hverr	hver	each
hverr	hver	who
in	hin	the
inn	hinn	the
íslenzkan	íslenskan	Icelander
jafnmjök	jafnmjög	equally-much

Old Norse	Old Icelandic	English
kæma	kæmi	come
kallat	kallað	called
kaupmaðr	kaupmaður	trading-man
kaupverðsins	skipverðsins	ship's-worth
kemr	kemur	came
kómu	komu	came
konungi	konungs	the-king
konungr	konungur	king
konungr	konungur	the-king
ksonungs	konungs	the-king's
lætr	lætur	behave
lætr	lætur	leave
lætr	lætur	let
leggr	leggur	laid
leitat	leitað	consider
lendr	lendur	land
lengr	lengur	longer
lézt	lést	had
liðit	liðið	passed
líðr	líður	passed
lítr	lítur	looked
litt	lítt	little
lízt	líst	appears
logizt	logist	cheated
lokit	lokið	ended
lýstr	lýstur	struck
maðr	maður	a-man
maðr	maður	man
mæðumst	mæðist	tired
mál	málið	matter
málagjöfna	málagjöfina	payment
málasilfrit	málasilfrið	silverware
margr	margur	many
mega	megi	may
mik	mig	me
mikit	mikið	huge
mjök	mjög	much
myndi	mundi	should
myndi	mundi	would
myndi	mundu	should
myndi	mundu	would
myndir	mundir	would
myndu	mundu	would

A Word Comparison of Old Norse and Old Icelandic

Old Norse	Old Icelandic	English	Old Norse	Old Icelandic	English
nætr	nætur	night	silfr	silfur	silver
náliga	nálega	nearly	silfrit	silfrið	the-silver
nauðgat	nauðgað	force	sitr	situr	sat
niðr	niður	below	sízt	síst	least
niðr	niður	down	sja	sjá	see
nökkur	nokkur	something	sjám	sjáum	we-see
nökkura	nokkura	some	skerit	skerið	a-rock
nökkurum	nokkurum	some	skilðust	skildust	separated
nökkut	nakkvað	something	skilaðr	skilnaður	parting
nökkut	nokkuð	something	skilr	skilur	separated
nökkut	nokkuð	somewhat	skipagangr	skipagangur	shipping
norðr	norður	north	skipit	skipið	ship
Nóreg	Noreg	Norway (place)	skipit	skipið	the-ship
Nóregi	Noregi	Norway (place)	skotit	skotið	launched
Nóregs	Noregs	Norway (place)	skyldi	skyldu	should
ófriðr	ófriður	un-peace	skyli	skuli	shall
ófúss	ófús	unwilling	skýtr	skýtur	launched
ok	og	also	sleitiliga	sleitilega	unfairly
ok	og	and	slótt	slóst	struck
okkr	okkur	our	spyrr	spyr	asked
okkr	okkur	us	stendr	stendur	stands
ómakliga	ómaklega	undeservedly	stendr	stendur	stood
ómjúkr	ómjúkur	un-bending	stórættaðr	stórættaður	of-high-family
ór	úr	from	stuttorðr	stuttorður	short-worded
ór	úr	out-of	stygglyndr	stygglyndur	quick-tempered
órráða	úrræða	solution	stýrimaðr	stýrimaður	steersman
óvingjarnliga	óvingjarnlega	unfriendly	styrkastr	styrkastur	strongest
prettum	prettunum	trick	suðr	suður	south
ráðit	ráðið	hired	sumarit	sumarið	summer
ræðr	ræður	leading	sundr	sundur	separate
rekit	rekið	thrown	svá	svo	so
sá	sáu	saw	sviviröliga	svívirðlega	dishonourable
sæmð	sæmd	honour	svívirðr	svívirður	dishonourable
sæmiligt	sæmilegt	the-same	tekit	tekið	taken
sér	sérð	see	tekr	tekur	took
sér	sért	be	þangat	þangað	from-there
setið	setjið	set	þat	það	it
síðr	síður	less	þat	það	that
Sigurðr	Sigurður	Sigurd (name)	þat	það	this
sik	sig	him	þatki	þatgi	that-not
			þik	þig	you

A Word Comparison of Old Norse and Old Icelandic

Old Norse	Old Icelandic	English	Old Norse	Old Icelandic	English
þjónat	þjónað	served	vill	vilt	wish
þykki	þyki	think	vingjarnlig	vingjarnleg	friendly
þykki	þykir	thought	vinr	vinur	friend
þykkir	þykir	seemed	vit	við	with
þykkir	þykir	thinks	vítishornit	vítishornið	penalty-horn
þykkist	þykist	think	vítit	vítið	penalty
þykkja	þykja	think	vítit	vítið	the-penalty
þykkjast	þykjast	consider	víttr	víttur	penalty
þykkjumst	þykist	think	víttr	víttur	reprimanded
tíðendi	tíðindi	tidings	vizkr	viskur	wise
tízka	tíska	custom	yðr	yður	you
undirhlutrinn	undirhluturinn	the-under-part	ykkarr	ykkar	with-you
unnit	unnið	deserved	ykkr	ykkur	you-two
upplenzkr	upplenskur	an-Upplander			
útan	utan	out			
vanði	vandi	custom			
vandskipaðr	vandskipaður	difficult			
vápndjarfastr	vopndjarfastur	weapons-bold			
vápnum	vopnum	weapons			
vár	vor	our			
vára	vora	going			
vára	vora	spring			
várit	vorið	spring			
várt	vort	ours			
váru	voru	were			
vátir	votir	wet			
váveifliga	voveiflega	unexpected			
vegr	vegur	way			
veizlum	veislum	the-feasts			
veizlur	veislur	feasts			
veizt	veist	know			
veiztu	veistu	know-you			
verðr	verður	came			
verðr	verður	worth			
verit	verið	be			
verit	verið	been			
verit	verið	being			
verit	verið	had-been			
vetr	vetur	winter			
vetrinn	veturinn	winter			
vili	vilji	willed			

www.ingramcontent.com/pod-product-compliance
Lightning Source LLC
Chambersburg PA
CBHW051420070526
44584CB00023B/3508